MARKET RESEARCH IN PRACTICE SERIES

Published in association with The Market Research Society
Consultant Editors: David Barr and Robin J Birn

Kogan Page has joined forces with The Market Research Society (MRS) to publish this unique series which is designed specifically to cover the latest developments in market research thinking and practice. Taking a practical, action-oriented approach, and focused on established 'need to know' subjects, the series will reflect the role of market research in the international business environment. This series will concentrate on developing practical texts on:

- how to use, act on and follow up research;
- research techniques and best practice.

Great effort has been made to ensure that each title is international in both content and approach and where appropriate, European, US and international case studies have been used comparatively to ensure that each title provides readers with models for research relevant to their own countries.

Overall the series will produce a body of work that will enhance international awareness of the MRS and improve knowledge of its Code of Conduct and guidelines on best practice in market research.

Other titles in the series:

Market Research in Practice: A guide to the basics, Paul Hague, Nick Hague and
    Carol-Ann Morgan
Market Intelligence: How and why organizations use market research, Martin
    Callingham

Forthcoming titles:

Questionnaire Design
Business to Business Market Research
Consumer Insight

To obtain further information, please contact the publisher at the address below:

Kogan Page Ltd
120 Pentonville Road
London N1 9JN
Tel: 020 7278 0433
www.kogan-page.co.

The Market Research Society

With over 8,000 members in more than 50 countries, The Market Research Society (MRS) is the world's largest international membership organization for professional researchers and others engaged in (or interested in) market, social and opinion research.

It has a diverse membership of individual researchers within agencies, independent consultancies, client-side organisations, and the academic community – at all levels of seniority and in all job functions.

All MRS members agree to comply with the MRS Code of Conduct (see Appendix), which is supported by the Codeline advisory service and a range of specialist guidelines on best practice.

MRS offers various qualifications and membership grades, as well as training and professional development resources to support these. It is the official awarding body in the UK for vocational qualifications in market research.

MRS is a major supplier of publications and information services, conferences and seminars, and many other meeting and networking opportunities for researchers.

MRS is 'the voice of the profession' in its media relations and public affairs activities on behalf of professional research practitioners, and aims to achieve the most favourable climate of opinion and legislative environment for research.

The Market Research Society (Limited by Guarantee) Company Number 518685

> Company Information: Registered office and business address:
> 15 Northburgh Street, London EC1V OJR
> Telephone: 020 7490 4911
> Fax: 020 7490 0608
> e-mail: info@marketresearch.org.uk
> Web site: www.mrs.org.uk

the EFFECTIVE USE of MARKET RESEARCH

HOW TO DRIVE AND FOCUS BETTER BUSINESS DECISIONS

ROBIN J BIRN

KOGAN PAGE

London & Sterling, VA

First published in Great Britain in 1988 by Kogan Page Limited
Revised and updated edition 1990
Second edition 1992
Third edition 1999
Fourth edition 2004

120 Pentonville Road
London N1 9JN
United Kingdom
www.kogan-page.co.uk

22883 Quicksilver Drive
Sterling VA 20166-2012
USA

© Robin J Birn, 1988, 1990, 1992, 1999, 2004

The right of Robin J Birn to be identified as the author of this work has been asserted by him in accordance with the Copyright, Designs and Patents Act 1988.

ISBN 0 7494 4200 X

British Library Cataloguing-in-Publication Data

A CIP record for this book is available from the British Library.

Library of Congress Cataloging-in-Publication Data

Birn, Robin.
  The effective use of market research: how to drive and focus better business decisions/Robin J. Birn. — 4th ed.
    p. cm.
  ISBN 0-7494-4200-X
1. Marketing research. 2. Decision making. 3. Strategic planning. 4. Success in business. I. Title
  HF5415.2.B49 2004
  658.8'3 — dc22   2004002754

Typeset by Datamatics Technologies Ltd, Mumbai, India
Printed and bound in Great Britain by Creative Print and Design (Wales), Ebbw Vale

Contents

Contents

The editorial board

CONSULTANT EDITORS

David Barr has been Director General of The Market Research Society since July 1997. He previously spent over 25 years in business information services and publishing. He has held management positions with Xerox Publishing Group, the British Tourist Authority and Reed International plc. His experience of market research is therefore all on the client side, having commissioned many projects for NPD and M&A purposes. A graduate of Glasgow and Sheffield Universities, David Barr is a Member of the Chartered Management Institute and a Fellow of The Royal Society of Arts.

Robin J Birn has been a marketing and market research practitioner for over 25 years. In 1985 he set up Strategy, Research and Action Ltd, which is now the largest international market research company for the map, atlas and travel guide sector, and the book industry. He is a Fellow of The Market Research Society and is also the editor of *The International Handbook of Market Research Techniques*.

ADVISORY MEMBERS

Martin Callingham was formerly Group Market Research Director at Whitbread, where he ran the Market Research department for 20 years and was a non-executive director of the company's German restaurant chain for more than 10 years. Martin has also played his part in the market research world. Apart from being on many committees of the MRS, of which he is a Fellow, he was Chairman of the Association of

Users of Research (AURA), has been a council member of ESOMAR, and has presented widely, winning the David Winton Award in 2001 at the MRS Conference.

Nigel Culkin is a Fellow of the Market Research Society and member of its Professional Development Advisory Board. He has been a full member since 1982. He has been in academia since 1991 and is currently Deputy Director, Commercial Development at the University of Hertfordshire, where he is responsible for activities that develop a culture of entrepreneurism and innovation among staff and students. He is Chair of the University's Film Industry Research Group (FiRG), supervisor to a number of research students and regular contributor to the media on the creative industries.

Professor Merlin Stone is Business Research Leader with IBM's Business Consulting Services, where he works on business research, consulting and marketing with IBM's clients, partners and universities. He runs the IBM Marketing Transformation Group, a network of clients, marketing agencies, consultancies and business partners, focusing on changing marketing. He is a director of QCi Ltd, an Ogilvy One company. Merlin is IBM Professor of Relationship Marketing at Bristol Business School. He has written many articles and 25 books on marketing and customer service, including *Up Close and Personal: CRM @ Work, Customer Relationship Marketing, Successful Customer Relationship Marketing, CRM in Financial Services* and *The Customer Management Scorecard*, all published by Kogan Page, and *The Definitive Guide to Direct and Interactive Marketing*, published by Financial Times-Pitman. He is a Founder Fellow of the Institute of Direct Marketing and a Fellow of the Chartered Institute of Marketing.

Paul Szwarc began his career as a market researcher at the Co-operative Wholesale Society (CWS) Ltd in Manchester in 1975. Since then he has worked at Burke Market Research (Canada), American Express Europe, IPSOS RSL, International Masters Publishers Ltd and PSI Global prior to joining the Network Research board as a director in October 2000. Over the past few years Paul has specialized on the consumer financial sector, directing multi-country projects on customer loyalty and retention, new product/service development, and employee satisfaction in the UK, European and North American markets. Paul is a full member of The Market Research Society. He has presented papers at a number of MRS and ESOMAR seminars and training courses.

Foreword

This revised and new edition of *The Effective Use of Market Research* has been written to fulfil a number of objectives. The key one relates to the positioning of research. Over the last 25 years of working in marketing and market research I have been constantly interested in the fact that many managers take decisions without research. There are also many managers who do not recognize that research would help them to make better decisions.

This situation indicates that the role, and to some extent the image, of market research is insufficiently clear, strong and focused as an important management tool. Market researchers believe that market research is important, but they have not been as successful as the advertising industry in communicating to management how it needs to depend on it. Nevertheless over the last few years there has been a change in the image of market research, and researchers are being seen as less of the technician and more of the problem solver and adviser.

This change is important for any organization because of the volume and extent of information. The digital age and development of databases have created greater awareness of information, but there has been an explosion of data to digest. Senior management will become progressively more dependent on analysis and interpretation of information, as the mechanisms for collecting data are further simplified through additional technological development.

So I felt it was important to demonstrate how fundamental marketing research is to the sales, marketing and communication process. It is also interesting to demonstrate the importance and relevance of marketing research to all levels of management, because if designed correctly, it can be used effectively. Marketing research can also provide management with a better insight into making sales, marketing and communications work, and assist in ensuring success.

This book clarifies the essential techniques of market research that management needs to know. It explains why research is needed, what it is and how companies that may not have used it much in the past become dependent on it. It clearly shows how market research helps to plan, focus and drive the marketing process and provide the necessary independent feedback on whether management is making the right or wrong decisions. It also shows the difference between the good and bad ways of doing market research, and the implications of not taking it on board effectively. I would also argue that it proves that it is the essential business tool that is required to make selling, marketing, advertising, promoting, distributing and all elements of customer service effective.

The Effective Use of Market Research has to be both useful and important to management in skills development. Marketing is all about satisfying customers. Research is all about getting the best feedback to ensure that customers are satisfied. A company that knows its customers and monitors its activity well, and has a good understanding of the key research techniques it needs, is likely to develop better and more competitive sales, marketing and communications strategies.

A company will grow its business if it is better equipped to approach its market with knowledge and understanding of customer needs, having confirmed what they like and dislike (and why), to help to target its products and services more effectively.

This new edition of *The Effective Use of Market Research* includes more case studies and information on how companies of any size can incorporate research into the decision making process. Our work over the last five years has concentrated on advising and training management on how to use both internal and external information, how to plan its analysis carefully and to know when additional research is needed. There is also a need to understand the legal framework of data protection and the professional ethics incorporated in the Market Research Society Code of Conduct. These determine the procedures that need to be adopted in collecting and analysing data professionally and legally.

Desk research has changed as a result of the Internet, and many more business people than have undertaken this role in the past are now involved in searching for information. But the 'information high-way' can be daunting to the manager seeking precise information, and guidance on how to search the Internet is essential.

The increasingly competitive environment in all market sectors also has impacted on research and how to complete it cost effectively. A company needs to be able to know the size of the markets it operates in, the market segments that it needs to focus on, and complete research that is representative of its current and potential customer base. Data analysis needs to be much more precise to provide feedback on performance in market segments and to give a company an indication of where to focus marketing and communications resources. It is therefore important to communicate research and data analysis precisely, and to find a format that all managers in a company can use to monitor market and marketing activities. Assessing the impact of the results of data analysis and research has become a more important role for managers, particularly for understanding what the data indicate in terms of how to take fast and effective actions. Using the data to know whether decisions are more effective than those being taken by competitors has become an essential role for research, and knowing competitive positioning can stimulate marketing and communications decisions effectively.

To conclude let me quote Derrick Mitchell, former Managing Director Sales and Marketing at Naturin GmbH & Co, with whom I have worked for 20 years. This is an interesting analogy he used in a seminar we were both running for his company's agents on how to use market research.

I am sure that we all remember the tale of Jack and the Beanstalk. Well, with a little stretch of the imagination you can also apply this fable to the market research process and the benefits accrued by a company such as ours.

You take your money to the market, discuss what to purchase with traders and buy a bean. This is like developing the core idea for research, deciding what you want to do and then spending money on it.

You take the bean home, plant it, nurture and nourish it and watch it grow. This is similar to developing the research hypothesis and specification, the brief, setting the samples for the research, the quotas for who to interview and developing the questionnaire, the analysis specification and agreeing all of this in management meetings.

When it has reached full maturity, it has grown so much that you can clamber through its branches and levels, revelling in the wonders and the clear view you have of everything. This is similar to having new knowledge as a result of the research and taking a different view on your sales and marketing issues.

So it is with market research – it is all about focusing the business and using knowledge, not guesswork.

Robin J Birn
Strategy, Research & Action Ltd
11 Warren Avenue
Richmond
Surrey TW10 5DZ
Tel: 020 8878 9482

Acknowledgements

We are such stuff as dreams are made of
and our little lives are rounded with a sleep.

William Shakespeare, *The Tempest*

Dreams can only be fulfilled if those who experience them, or even 'appear' in them, take decisions that allow them to replicate the ideas, thoughts and situations in reality. Many people feel that their lives are more meaningful if their sleep is interrupted or, as some say, made more interesting with a dream in the middle. Whatever the experience of a person with a dream, it stands as an example that can be followed or, for those who have unpleasant ones, avoided.

Managers are always interested in fulfilling dreams because they are eager to follow examples demonstrated by situations in other companies. It is the way in which they believe they can become more creative in their decision making, taking the example of others to achieve the dreams they want to achieve for their own companies.

Authors are also dependent on experiences to make their books the dreams that can be achieved by the reader. However, when writing business books, the authors are more likely to relate experiences shared with colleagues, friends and companies with whom work has been completed. It is only through the medium of written communications that an opportunity to express true appreciation for the interest and support that is realized in such a project as this can be expressed with the gratitude it deserves. I therefore want to be able to say how I appreciate the opportunities we have had in the last 25 years, when some of what follows in this book has been realized and developed by those we have had pleasure to work with.

Specific appreciation must be expressed too to a number of people who have been involved in some form or other that has given me the time, resource and support to write this book. I first want to thank my whole family, Danit, Daniel and David for their support in giving me time to write the book, sometimes early in the morning before the school run, sometimes late at night after the homework. They have also been tremendous with expressing their further support for the very heavy international travelling schedule that has become part of my working life over the last 20 years 'fulfilling the dreams'. This schedule also gave me time to write parts of the original version of this book at 38,000 feet with the world's favourite airline looking after me, with those passengers sitting next to me irritated that they could not talk because I was busy writing a chapter.

Others have also been involved in helping to review how research can grow business and be effective in the working environment, but have really made the ideas work in practice. Derrick Mitchell has been interested in the application of a series of the ideas in the book, particularly the 'win-win' theory. With his humour, company on many trips across the world and enthusiasm for developing hypotheses that have been effectively proved, it has added much pleasure to all of this work. And I also appreciate the contributions he has made in a number of places in the book.

Members of the publishing industry also need special mention, as they have been totally supportive for many years. In the UK they include Mike Cranidge, David Croom and Patrick Forsyth, and in the United States Bill Hunt, John Coerper, John Szal, Karen Davis, Bill Stoehr, Howard Danley and Gavin Maurer. Our work in the United States has also given me the proud opportunity to really enjoy my US dual nationality thanks to my father – and I am particularly pleased that Kogan Page is publishing this book in the United States too.

For 17 of the 25 years I have worked as a volunteer worker for the Market Research Society, serving on a number of committees, the Council for eight years and as Vice-Chairman for two years. I am proud to have been appointed a Fellow of the Market Research Society, and this gives me the opportunity to thank many research industry colleagues I have worked with on projects that have helped to develop the positioning of research. My Fellowship will be used to continue to do what I can to communicate the use of research to the publishing industry and developing membership of the Society.

1 Key to making good decisions

INTRODUCTION

Fifty years ago, before the market research industry existed, all management took decisions without systematic market analysis or information. Markets and economies were in a different mode and the world was trying to come to terms with its political structure. After World War II the economies of the modern era decided to find new opportunities. Gradually the new-found techniques of political and social research were developed, and market and marketing research became a management tool in major corporations.

The 1960s saw a new phase of marketing, using the market segmentation approach, as manufacturers became aware that they had to become closer to the 'markets within markets' and the different characteristics of consumers within a defined market. The 1970s saw the growth of product development and techniques for evaluating the success of communication. The early 1980s were heralded by an increase in the amount of research carried out by service companies. The results of this helped a new trend to emerge in the use of research techniques at the end of the 1980s. Monitoring customer service has become a definitive trend of how companies are using research to determine objectively whether they are doing their jobs well or badly in the eyes of the consumer.

Marketing in the 1990s was characterized by further innovation through product differentiation and service development. Consumers are becoming older, more pragmatic and more discerning. Marketing emphasizes the 'psycho-graphic' aspects, focusing specifically on their lifestyles and how their needs differ. In the new century it has become more important to understand the different habits of the various types of customers or consumers, and keep a competitive edge in meeting their constantly changing needs.

In research terms this has seen an increasing dependence on proven techniques, as they have been established in providing information which management needs. What is interesting is the fact that more managers in companies are becoming more dependent on using research techniques, as companies become totally 'information oriented' on the 'information highway'. The computer age has exposed more management teams to information than in the past, and because of the volume and flow of information in a company, it will become more and more important for management to know how to collect it, collate it, store it, interpret it, analyse it and understand the implications of the facts contained within it. The analysis of data now needs to 'work for them' more than in the past.

It is therefore essential that management clearly understands what information is and why it is important to take decisions based on facts rather than assumptions. It is also clear that those who do use information for decision making also realize that they take better decisions as a result of using data. The implications of this for management are:

- better knowledge of their markets and the customers they are selling to;
- more focused decisions and plans that are realistic to the market;
- decisions that are based on more cost effective sales, marketing and communications methods;
- decisions that assist the company to increase sales by ensuring that customer needs are met and satisfied;
- acting on the research that is completed.

Information therefore is the key to taking good decisions as it enhances the decision making process. However, to ensure this is done effectively the meaning of both information and decisions has to be evaluated.

WHAT INFORMATION IS

The real definition of information, as given by the *Oxford Concise Dictionary*, is:

- informing;
- knowledge;
- news.

Research encompasses all of these factors if the breadth of research is appreciated. Information through the adoption of research techniques has a fundamental *informing* role for management. It relates facts about a product or market, which the manager may or may not already know. Research always improves the *knowledge* of management, as managers need to understand clearly what the needs of the customers are and how these needs are always changing. Research also provides plenty of *news*, as a well designed research project will provide facts or facets of situations not clear to management that it is not likely to have known before.

Information, therefore, is something on which management should depend for making good decisions. It is vital in the decision making process, and so key that it is difficult to understand how companies take decisions without information. But many managers will agree that they do.

WHY TAKE DECISIONS WITH INFORMATION?

Researchers say that decision making cannot be done effectively without a continuous flow of marketing information and research – it is the trends that matter. Information on your customers and how well you are marketing to them is:

- a reassurance that you know who they are;
- a source of feedback on how well you are servicing them;
- key to knowing the changes in the market;
- key to knowing how to make customers loyal in the longer term.

The onus is therefore on management to decide what information is needed to make sure that the decision taken is improved through the use of information. Management needs to be able to decide:

- What data or information is needed?
- Which decisions will be influenced by this information?
- How is the information to be collected?
- How is the information to be analysed?
- What expenditure is required to collect the information?
- How can a decision be taken without the information?
- Is a wrong decision likely to be taken as a result of not having the information?

The questions above are designed to make the manager think through the need for information, define how it will be used, assess the alternatives of having or not having the information, and finally decide the course of action for the decision making process. This, in essence, is a structural approach to decision making. It is a means of deciding in advance what is required from information collection, rather than taking a decision without the facts. It prevents the taking of a decision without an interpretation, which is more robust than a professional judgement.

Later in the book we shall also see that the better the preparation for the research, the better the result that is achieved. We shall also review the opinions of users of research who have had success in using it. Assessment of the information that is needed shapes the nature of the exploratory processes that have to be conducted through market research. Information therefore gives direction to decision making.

CASE STUDY

A contract hire company: making meetings shorter by using good information

This company which learnt how to use information to improve its decisions is in the contract hire sector, providing trucks, cranes, cement mixers and any other equipment required on a building site. The management committee of the company met every month to discuss its activities. The meetings included members of the board, sales management, marketing management, production management and research and development management. Ten days prior to the meeting each of the personnel who were to attend were required to submit a report of their activities in the previous month. At the meeting each manager read his report, which only listed what he or she had done in the last month. The Finance Director prepared an analysis of computer data, tabled at the meeting only, which showed:

- the monthly sales analysis, as an analysis of the sales of each company in the group;
- a comparison with the sales in the same month in the previous year;
- a comparison with the agreed sales targets for the month.

There was no analysis of the trends in the data and information being discussed, so many of the meetings became repetitive in the managers' interpretation of the information. There was little discussion about the impact of the information on the adopted strategy, and whether results were better or worse than expected.

Readers of this book may find this company familiar, in that its situation is similar to their own. There is nothing wrong with the approach of this company, as it had functioned this way for a very long time. What was wrong was management's failure to use the meeting for better planning, and to identify how data on the company's performance could help to develop and improve its future performance.

Decisions in this company were taken from the exchange of 'collected intelligence' collated by managers talking to each other, talking to their staff and talking to their customers. This is essentially not a systematic process. There was little reference to external market data or more detailed information, and the data were not analysed to produce a long-term trend analysis.

So changes had to be made. The changes that took place, which are easily implemented in any company provided management allocates the time to set up the systems, required the management to become much more involved in the specification and interpretation of the information. Over a period of three months the company accountant produced customized computer material, designed to give management feedback on the discussions at the monthly meeting. The format of this data was much more detailed than before, and initially there was concern that there would be more information than could be analysed, digested and understood by the management committee. As these factors were important to a group of managers who were not accustomed to using data, it was agreed only to use this information in the monthly meetings, and to use it in a graphical format, which could be easily interpreted.

Each division of the company was provided with a graphical analysis of data, which showed the sales budget for the division over the last two years on a month-by-month basis, and the actual sales for the division over the same period. This gave the managers an immediate visual analysis of their performance. Not only did it confirm whether sales were on target or not, it defined a 'trend' analysis as to whether the trend of current performance was overall positive or negative.

After three months, as all the managers became used to the system, more information was introduced. The graphical analysis was enhanced by adding information on the various divisions' types of customer and market segments. This new data therefore provided a further management control, in that it identified trends within customer types, and helped to determine which customer groups needed to be targeted for additional sales activity or customer servicing.

The contract hire company therefore became more 'market oriented' in its decision making, and was making better use of internal sales statistics.

HOW INFORMATION IMPROVES DECISIONS

Information becomes vital to the decision making process when it is well prepared, used pragmatically, and analysed and interpreted with 'market-led' implications. It improves the decision making process by reducing uncertainty, as well as reducing the number of assumptions that a team of managers might take. Information therefore allows a more systematic assessment of the facts about a market, or product, or any decisions managers take. The keys to making good decisions therefore are to use information, become more analytical in the way it is interpreted, and become dependent on taking a decision when there are facts to support it.

Many companies find it difficult to recognize that information will assist them. Typically their personnel have worked in them for some time, and the managers have become used to making 'informed decisions'. Readers of this book may find that they have to persuade their colleagues to use information at all. But trends are developing for the increasing use of information, and this book helps to define what key information is needed to develop the business.

A marketing director of a major food company has said to his management, 'No self-deception, be honest. You may try to deceive others. But if there is a problem you cannot ignore it. It is important if the consumer sees a problem.'

WHY IT IS IMPORTANT TO USE DATA AND RESEARCH

Customers' needs are always changing, competitors' activities are always changing and the market environment in which business operates changes because of external factors, such as political and economic circumstances that result from tax changes, terrorism and international relations. Managers have become more focused as companies operate leaner and more efficient organizations, and they cannot keep an intimate knowledge of their customers and their needs because of pressure of time.

Data and research therefore has become more essential to help to monitor change and provide managers with an 'early warning system' on how to keep customers satisfied. But our experience has shown that many companies find it difficult to find time to plan their data analysis and data collection carefully, and a specific project team or activity needs to be put in place to make this happen. It is important for all managers in a company to adopt the traditional marketing planning skills of developing a strategy, testing and monitoring it, to find time to understand their markets and customers better. It is effective to convene a management team and review the following questions:

- Where are we now?
- Where do we want to go?
- And how do we get there?

Answering these questions will give management the chance to take a step back and identify whether it is meeting market and customers needs effectively. It will also assist in deciding on priorities for marketing and communications activities in the future, and in getting them into the context of change that is constant and affects all decisions.

BRAINSTORMS AND WORKSHOPS ARE EFFECTIVE

Our experience has been to work with managers to facilitate this discussion process and to challenge their views of their own marketing activities, how to respond to change and how to become more market focused. It is an effective technique to convene a marketing workshop or 'brainstorm' session, as it gives a chance for management in a company to become involved in the decisions that will contribute to future success.

Many managers find it difficult to conceptualize what data and information is needed to help them answer the three traditional questions, so it is important to review other questions to develop the discussion. The following are effective, provided each manager answers the questions in relation to his or her own role in the company and then participates in a review to consolidate the answers, so that a company develops its consensus view of what are the key answers that need to be addressed:

- What do we know about our markets and customers?
- What do we want to know about our markets and customers?
- What data and information are essential to assist us in the decisions that we need to take to be successful?

■ What data and information are essential to assist us to know that we are more successful than competitors and that we are keeping our customers satisfied?

Our experience shows that management teams answering these questions agree that they are not as close to their customers as they had thought, and that they need to use data and information more effectively in their companies. They recognize that they do not analyse their own internal customer and sales data effectively, to help them to monitor success and identify change. They recognize that they do not develop data that helps them to test out their market and product development ideas, or check out whether customers believe they are providing a better product or service than competitors. And they recognize that they need to be more analytical in their approach to decision making.

Completing this process is also effective for internal success. Senior management is more likely to be favourable to change, and investment in time and resources to analyse internal data and collect external data, if there is a definitive need to monitor change and understand markets and customers. It becomes more obvious how the data will assist in decision making.

DATA PROTECTION AND GOOD PRACTICE

All businesses and managers need to be aware of the increasing amount of legislation and regulation that impacts on the use of data and research. This relates primarily to transparency, privacy and confidentiality of data.

Data protection in the UK

There are two important elements concerning data protection and good practice of which any UK company involved in analysing data and completing market research should be aware. They are the Data Protection Act 1998 and the Market Research Society Code of Conduct.

The Data Protection Act is concerned with the fundamental rights of individuals who are asked for, or provide, information about themselves. Its core principles are transparency and consent. Transparency involves ensuring that individuals have a very clear and unambiguous understanding of the purpose(s) for collecting the data and how it will be used. At the time that the data is collected, individuals must give their consent to its collection, and also at this time they must be given the opportunity to opt out of any subsequent uses of the data.

In the case of market research this means ensuring that it is clearly spelt out to respondents at the beginning of the interview that the information collected will only be used for confidential survey research purposes, and that if a further interview is likely to be necessary, permission for this must be granted during the initial interview.

Article 1 of the EU Data Protection Directive requires member states to 'protect the fundamental rights and freedoms of natural persons, and in particular their right to privacy with respect to the processing of personal data'. The 1998 Act represents the UK implementation of revised data protection legislation to meet this overall objective. Reference to this Act and to the Market Research Society Code of Conduct provides any organization with guidelines that need to be taken into account, including specific issues that apply to company databases.

The eight core principles within the Act are shown below. The British Standards Institution Guide to the Practical Implementation of the 1998 Act describes these as the 'rules of the game' – the fundamental basis of the legislation. These principles are also included within the current MRS Code of Conduct, and all members have to become familiar with them and what they imply:

- Personal data shall be processed fairly and lawfully and, in particular, shall not be processed unless at least one of the conditions in Schedule 2 of the Act is met, and in the case of sensitive personal data, at least one of the conditions in Schedule 3 is also met.
- Personal data shall be obtained only for one or more specified and lawful purposes, and shall not be further processed in any manner incompatible with that purpose or other purposes.
- Personal data shall be adequate, relevant and not excessive in relation to the purpose or purposes for which they are processed.
- Personal data shall be accurate and, where necessary, kept up to date (with every reasonable step being taken to ensure that data that are inaccurate or incomplete, having regard to the purpose(s) for which they were collected or for which they are being further processed, are erased or rectified).

- Personal data processed for any purpose or purposes shall not be kept for longer than is necessary for that purpose or those purposes.
- Personal data shall be processed in accordance with the rights of data subjects under the Act.
- Appropriate technical and organizational measures shall be taken against unauthorized or unlawful processing of personal data and against accidental loss or destruction of, or damage to, personal data.
- Personal data shall not be transferred to a country or territory outside the European Economic Area unless that country or territory ensures an adequate level of protection for the rights and freedoms of data subjects in relation to the processing of personal data.

Those engaged in market research, on all sides of the industry, are increasingly developing or using databases containing personal data either to hold information or as sampling frames. Data protection legislation in many countries places increased responsibilities on data controllers to ensure that databases are properly managed.

The EU Directive instructs that data controllers should comply with the law of the EU state in which the controller is located and in which processing is carried out. When the controller is responsible for and/or located in several EU countries, then he/she must ensure that they comply with the laws of all member states in which data processing takes place.

All members of the Market Research Society must adhere to the MRS Code of Conduct when conducting market research. The MRS Code of Conduct is designed to support all those engaged in marketing or social research in maintaining professional standards. It applies to all members of the MRS whether they are engaged in consumer, business-to-business, social opinion or any other type of confidential survey research. The MRS Code of Conduct does not take precedence over national law. The Code of Conduct and Guidelines can be reviewed on www.mrs.org.uk/code.htm.

Data protection in the United States

Data protection is dealt with in the United States very differently from how it is dealt with in Europe, as the procedures are fundamental to the legislative framework. The First and Fourth Amendments of the US Constitution, as well as consumer protection laws, grant limited privacy rights. In addition there are about 90 data privacy bills in the US Congress, mainly intended to protect children and medical records. The Children's Online Privacy Protection Act, passed by the US Congress in October 1998, requires Web site operators to obtain parental consent before obtaining personal information from children, and the Consumer Internet Privacy Protection Act requires an Internet service provider to get permission from a subscriber before disclosing his or her personal information to third parties.

However existing federal laws do not yet suffice to cover the broad range of issues and circumstances that make the new digital environment a threat to personal privacy. The US Government has also been reluctant to impose a regulatory burden on electronic commerce activities that could hamper their development and has looked for an answer in self-regulation.

The elaboration of Codes of Conduct by independent associations has proliferated in recent years, as a means of persuading companies to take the necessary steps towards ensuring the proper handling of personal data. Self-regulation is commercially driven, and it is often the case that the privacy policy a company claims to offer is simply not respected.

The Federal Trade Commission (FTC) undertook a study on the effectiveness of self-regulation over data protection following hearings in June 1997. The FTC declared that industry self-regulation had 'fallen far short of what is needed', and issued its online privacy recommendations on 4 June 1998, after finding out that the vast majority of Web sites processing data about their visitors did not follow any privacy policy at all. The FTC then put forth four information practice principles that should be addressed by companies undertaking personal data processing:

- **notice:** how data is collected;
- **choice:** whether it will be used or not;
- **access:** to an individual's own data, in order to ensure accuracy;
- **security:** of the personal data process itself.

The FTC stated that online privacy policies would satisfy its guidelines if they stated:

- what is collected;
- for what purpose;

■ what necessary steps are undertaken to protect confidentiality quality and integrity; and

■ the rights of redress available to individuals.

In the United States there is also the Marketing Research Association's Code of Marketing Research Standards, which was established to ensure that MRA members conform to the following principles:

■ Conduct research in an honest and ethical manner.

■ Instill confidence in research and encourage public cooperation.

■ Instill confidence that research is done in a professional and fair manner.

■ Carry out every research project in accordance with the Code.

■ Respect the general public and its rights.

The principles of this Code are adhered to and signed by each member of the Marketing Research Association, both corporate and individual, as a condition of membership. Non-members of the MRA are encouraged to familiarize themselves with this Code to facilitate their dealing with MRA members and as an educational tool.

The Marketing Research Association is a recognized leader in the opinion and marketing research industry, advancing practical application, use and understanding of the opinion and marketing research profession. A fundamental aim of the Association is to ensure that standards are maintained. It is important that opinion and marketing research knowledge and the value of research are communicated to both the business community and the public at large, while complying with applicable federal, state and local laws, regulations and ordinances.

The MRA expects members to follow principles of honesty, professionalism, fairness and confidentiality to guard the interests of the public and clients in order to promote good business practices. The MRA's Code of Marketing Research Standards addresses the responsibilities of its members, not only to each other, but also to the general public and business community (see www.mra-net.org/codes/index.cfm).

Worldwide differences in data protection legislation

This is a brief overview of the main items of data protection legislation:

United States

Health Insurance Portability and Accountability Act (HIPAA) 1996
Gramm, Leach, Bliley Act 1999

Australia

Privacy Amendment Act 2000

Canada

Personal Information Protection and Electronic Documents Act

Hong Kong

Principle 4 Security of Personal Data

Japan

Privacy of Personal Data

New Zealand

Principle 5 Security of Personal Information

United Kingdom

Data Protection Act 1998

European Union

European Union Council Personal Data.

HINTS ON TAKING GOOD DECISIONS

The following are hints on how information helps to make good decisions:

- Avoid having meetings in which decisions are taken without using any company data.
- Avoid taking decisions based on past experiences. Markets and customer needs are always changing, and information is vital to indicate when these changes are happening.
- To help to decide on priorities for collecting information, regularly ask:

- Where are we now?
- Where do we want to go?
- How do we get there?

■ Extract the data needed to monitor key existing markets and customer groups, but do not generate more data than can be digested and understood quickly from the computer.

■ Customize the data by making it presentable in a graphic format, which can be easily accessed, interpreted and most importantly updated.

■ Use the information to plot 'trends' in market and customer groups, and allow all management to be influenced by the data.

■ Review and revise the format of the data analysis to ensure that the information system is 'dynamic' in relation to the management team's needs.

■ Check out the increasing amount of legislation that has an impact on the use of data and research. It is important to have a good understanding of the Market Research Society Code of Conduct and the regulatory environment on data protection.

■ Good decisions are information-based. Information is only effective if it is used to indicate whether decisions are right or wrong. The key to making good decisions is to learn how to use information effectively.

2 Getting the information you really need

INTRODUCTION

Using market research information is a management discipline, which needs to be learnt, developed and integrated into a manager's greater understanding of how to manage effectively. Some managers who use research have been heard to say that they spent time and resources collecting the information, but when it had been collected it was just 'a piece of information on which they could not act'. It is these managers who have failed to design, set up and implement the research well. They have failed to be imaginative with their need for information – only using it to prove or disprove their ideas or just to collect new information. Collecting information in isolation is also likely to be an ineffective research method, as the information obtained is unlikely to relate to the business or management problems.

Market research injects a flow of data and information into a company. It is constantly collected and it is not always analysed well. Extracting this data from the company's databases is as important as collecting it. The key to getting the information a manager really needs – inputting and extracting the essential data – is to develop a marketing information system.

A marketing information system – a MIS – coordinates the collection and extraction process and helps to develop a databank of information that is used and acted on. The implication of using a marketing information system is that the company is likely to be more market oriented, using data to guide the decision making process. In fact a system will:

- Control the amount of information a company needs. Efficient system management will ensure that the company collects and uses the data it needs.
- Need regular evaluation to help management to decide on its needs or data.
- Be dependent on the computer systems and the use of computer software to make it effective through database marketing and the like.
- Need to be supplemented with both ad hoc survey research data and continuous and 'one-off' problem solving data. Survey information such as this is essential for managers to gain a better understanding of the markets in which they operate, as well as the success of their decisions.
- Become the 'centre of excellence' for the company, the focal point for information, intelligence and statistical background that managers need.
- Help to guide managers in competitive decisions for the effective allocation of marketing, sales and communications resources.

A marketing information system will help a company get the information it really needs as it educates managers in what:

- information is essential;
- is happening with current and potential customers;
- data is interesting, but not key to the operating management process.

Marketing information systems therefore make a significant contribution to making research effective in assisting increasing sales.

HOW TO SET UP SYSTEMS

Getting the information you really need depends on the company analysing its customers and markets, as this is crucial for the success of sales activities. Companies are finding that customers are becoming more expensive to reach, and therefore it is even more vital to identify the target audiences clearly.

Managers may have experienced the analysis of data only by reading the current reports from their research suppliers. Typically, because of the main emphasis of market research, this process would usually relate to a product launch or an evaluation of a specific marketing problem. The advantage of a marketing information system is that users can make use of data whenever they need to. Now, with further technological development, data is becoming more available wherever managers are working.

The marketing information system is divided into two, as is shown in Tables 2.1 and 2.2. Table 2.1 shows the market research content of the system, defining the desk research and the survey research. Table 2.2 shows the information needed for monitoring marketing planning, and defining what information assists in setting marketing objectives, marketing strategies and evaluating marketing tactics.

The task for managers when determining how to set up a marketing information system is to decide the following:

- What range of data analysis functions are likely to be needed?
  - What market segments exist?
  - What proportion of the market is our customers?
  - What statistical and regression analysis is needed for market and product development?
  - If representative of the market and if developed into a model, what effective forecasting techniques can be used?
- Can data be imported from other systems – financial, sales, and other operational data – to define the market?
- What is the volume of data that is needed? Will the system be able to cope with the data? Can it be updated easily?
- What data output is needed and how can it be put together for ease of interpretation?
- Who is going to use the data? And how are they going to use it?
- What frequency of information is needed to provide good data for management reporting?

If these factors are evaluated carefully, a marketing information system will be well designed, but it has to be 'customized' to a company to be effective. A well designed system will enhance decisions, as they will be better informed. It will help to give a manager a clearer understanding of a company's competitive positioning and its market share. But more importantly, it will improve a manager's ability to identify opportunities and trends in the market. The key element for managers is that they will be able to identify who the customers of the company are, what their buying trends are and what they are likely to want to buy. An automated marketing information system will therefore bring market research closer to a wider range of managers, to help guide their decisions. Output from the system will ensure that managers are well informed about their markets, which will ensure that they take more focused decisions about market development and sales in the future.

The 1990s began with the firm establishment of information technology as a sales and marketing tool for better analysis. A survey by a leading management consultancy showed that 70 per cent of companies believe that a marketing database is more important than ever before. In the new century most companies depend on their marketing database, but they may not be analysing the data effectively.

Managers are saying that the benefits of these systems are cost savings and increased sales and profitability. However the survey also gives some important information on the problems managers have experienced in setting up the systems. The rank order of these problems, from most to least important, is:

- poorly defined requirements;
- a gulf between the marketing and information and technology staff, not understanding each other's needs clearly;
- lack of management commitment;
- lack of sufficient financial resources;
- lack of experience of the potential users of the systems and problems with systems interfacing within the company;
- lack of interest in using the system;
- lack of ability to analyse data.

Marketing information systems are now becoming essential in competitive markets for efficient information management. More and more managers have an improved understanding of how an MIS can be used to support a sales and marketing activity. The result of this is value for money in using information and a better chance of success in monitoring market trends and the needs of customers.

Table 2.1 *Marketing information system 1: market research content*

	Desk research	**Survey research**
Quantitative information	Market size Volumes of sales Annual trends Seasonal trends 'State of health' of the market	Demographics of customers and potential customers: – owners – users – buyers Products used and preferred Price paid Purchasing habits Lifestyle and background
Qualitative information	Market trends Performance of products Active/inactive segments Competitor activity Technological development	Consumer needs Consumer attitudes Consumer preferences Attitudes and motivations towards: – products – prices – promotions – advertising – future purchase Comparative competitive evaluation

Table 2.2 *Marketing information system 2: information needed for monitoring marketing planning*

	Marketing objectives	**Marketing strategies**	**Marketing tactics**
Quantitative information	Quarterly sales Quarterly trends	Product tracking Market tracking	Sales tracking Advertising tracking
	Annual sales	Competitive tracking	Promotion tracking
	Quarterly potential		
	Annual potential		
	Current market share		
	Potential market share		
	Quarterly profit		
	Annual profit		
Qualitative information	Reasons for: – trends	Market penetration	Attitude to products
	– sales – potentials	New market opportunity	Assessment of prices
	– market share – profitability	New product opportunity	Evaluation of advertising
		New ideas	Evaluation of direct marketing
		Diversifying the business	Evaluation of promotions
			Assessment of sales support
			Assessment of training and back-up and other resources

INTERNAL DATA NEEDED IN THE SYSTEM

Information technology has had the effect of involving more and more managers in the use of marketing information and research, and encouraging them to become more analytical. Establishing a marketing information system will mean that managers now deal with market data, prospect data and customer data.

Internally, a marketing information system needs to collect, coordinate and disseminate all aspects of internal operating data. This data is the 'marketing intelligence' of a company, and it is the control that managers need to run an effective sales and marketing operation. But getting the information that is really needed from a marketing information system depends on what the information is and how it is used. The following internal operating data are essential:

- Sales data, presented in a graphic format, can provide regular sales trend information and highlight whether certain customer types need to be targeted or focused.
- Price information by product line, compared with competitors, can monitor market trends; analysed by customer type, it can check price trends in customer groups.
- Stock level data and trends in key accounts or distributors, focusing on whether different outlets need support, provide market share information.
- Marketing support information, coordinating the effects of marketing promotions, through advertising, direct marketing, trade incentives, consumer competitions and so on, helps to determine whether decisions are being made effectively.
- Competitive information, reviewing competitors' promotions and communications to see if the company is doing it better or worse than competitors, can improve market targeting.

Every company setting up a marketing information system must customize the data that is entered into the system. Managers must also agree the format of its output, to ensure they understand it, can discuss it and can use it for effective sales and marketing planning.

Some managers would probably see the development of a marketing information system as a company information technology project. If this is so, then there are clear guidelines as to how the project should be completed to be successful. They are as follows.

Good communications

It is important that the sales and marketing staff and the information and technology staff know what is happening in the project and are clear as to the use of the system.

Commitment needs to be available from all levels of management

Development of such a system is likely to change the culture of the company, as decisions will be taken in a different manner. It is therefore important that all managers work in unison on the project, and that the lead is taken particularly by senior management. This means at the start of the project that the goals to be achieved are identified, discussed, prioritized and actioned, and that everyone works together to achieve these goals.

Run the project using an agreed plan

It is important to agree a 'critical path' for the project, so that no tasks are forgotten.

Decide on what data is needed

Committing the company to data output before the system is set up and development begins will ensure that the data is published and used by all managers who are involved in strategic and task based decisions.

THE EXTERNAL DATA THAT IS NEEDED

Whatever marketing intelligence information or internal operating data is needed by a management team, data collected internally is likely to have gaps in it. Opportunities are bound to be identified for additional information, such as data that is not automatically coming into the company but that, if accessed, will enhance the decision making process.

It is important for a company to 'map' the market in which it exists, to understand the structure of the market and its marketing positioning within it. The questions that need to be answered in order to develop a customized market map are:

- What is the size of the market in terms of value and volume?
- What is the shape of the market in the context of the distribution structure and intermediaries?
- Are the trends for an increasing, static or declining market?
- What is the nature of the competition and how does our company differ from them?
- Which customers buy, what do they prefer, and which other buying groups are potential customers?
- What is the 'lifestyle' of the customers and what is their typical buying pattern?
- Which sales, marketing and communications methods are used and which of these are successful?
- How satisfied are customers with the company's products and services and how does this compare with competitors?

However, a management team that is interested in using market research to increase business needs to evaluate what aspects of external data should be collected to supplement the internal information. This relates specifically to:

- defining where we are now, where we want to go and how we get there;
- setting the company's marketing objectives, to achieve the goals;
- segmenting the market and understanding the priorities for the different segments;
- defining the essential strategies to approach the market;
- establishing effective tactics to implement the strategic marketing plan.

Initially it is important to install in the marketing information system all the basic sources of information on the market in which the company is operating. Checking these sources of information is essential, as it may identify free or low-cost data sources, and save the company money if it currently carries out surveys to collect the same data.

SOURCES OF INFORMATION

The following sources of information are usually included. Most governments issue a vast array of official statistical data, which can be highly relevant primary sources, and may also form the basis for constructing samples for survey research. The following lists from the UK and United States give an indication of the type of information that is in the public domain. Much of it is readily accessible not only in conventional hard-copy format, but also from online sources.

UK government statistical publications

The Office of National Statistics publishes the following data, which can be accessed via www.statistics.gov.uk:

Agriculture, fishing and forestry

Agriculture census by geographical area
Agriculture in the United Kingdom
Economic report on Scottish agriculture
Farm incomes in the United Kingdom
National food survey
Scottish sea fisheries statistics

Commerce, energy and industry

Assets and liabilities of finance houses and other consumer credit grantors
Business spending on capital items
Computer services survey
Insurance companies', pension funds' and trusts' investments – motor vehicle production inquiry
PRODCOM annual industry reports 2001
PRODCOM annual industry reports 2000
PRODCOM annual industry reports 1999
Quality review of the inter-departmental business register
Research and development in UK businesses
Size analysis of United Kingdom businesses
Small and medium enterprises
The UK service sector

Compendia and reference

2000 annual report of the Registrar General for Scotland
60 years of social survey 1941–2001
Annual abstract
Britain update
Digest of Welsh historical statistics
Electoral statistics, Scotland 2002
ESRC review of government social classifications
Fact card guide to sources
Focus on London 2000
Guide to official statistics 2000
Living in Britain
Monthly digest of statistics
Region in figures –2002
Regional trends
Scottish economic statistics
Social survey methodological bulletin
The official yearbook of the United Kingdom
The Scottish abstract of statistics (1998)
Tracking people: a guide to longitudinal social sources
UK standard industrial classification volumes 1 and 2 (2003)

Crime and justice

Drug-related deaths in Scotland in 2000
The 2000 British crime survey

Economy

Aerospace and electronics cost indices
Consumer price indices
Consumer trends
Economic trends
Economic trends: digest of articles
Financial statistics
Financial statistics explanatory handbook
Focus on consumer price indices
Foreign direct investment
Household satellite account
Input–output tables and multipliers for Scotland

Monthly review of external trade statistics
Price index numbers for current cost accounting
Producer price indices
Productivity
Retail sales
Scottish economic statistics
Scottish local government financial statistics
Share ownership
UK trade in services
UK regional trade statistics
United Kingdom balance of payments – the pink book
United Kingdom economic accounts
United Kingdom national accounts, concepts, sources and methods
United Kingdom national accounts – the blue book
United Kingdom trade in goods analysed in terms of industry

Education and training

Scottish education statistics
Student achievement in England
Student achievement in Northern Ireland

Health and care

Abortion statistics, 1999–2000
Adult dental health survey
Adults with a psychotic disorder living in private households
Cancer statistics – registrations, England
Cancer trends in England and Wales 1950–1999
Child health statistics
Children and adolescents who try to harm, hurt or kill themselves
Congenital anomaly statistics – 2001 and earlier editions
Contraception and sexual health
Department of Health on-line statistical products
Drinking: adults' behaviour and knowledge
General pharmaceutical services
Geographic variations in health
Health and personal social services statistics for England
Health inequalities decennial supplement
Health statistics quarterly

ISD Scotland – Scottish health statistics online
Key health statistics from general practice
Life expectancy by health and local authorities in the UK
Mental health of carers
Mortality statistics – cause
Mortality statistics – childhood infant and prenatal
Mortality statistics – injury and poisoning
Mortality statistics – general
National congenital anomaly system
Non-fatal suicidal behaviour among adults aged 16–74
Psychiatric morbidity among adults living in private households
Psychiatric morbidity among prisoners in England and Wales
Scottish health care
Smoking-related behaviour and attitudes
Studies on medical and population subjects
The mental health of children and adolescents in Great Britain
The social and economic circumstances of adults with mental disorders
Tobacco, alcohol and drug use and mental health
United Kingdom health statistics
Vacancy monitoring report – residential care homes and nursing homes
in Scotland
Young teenagers and smoking

Labour market

Annual local area labour force survey summary publication
Guide to labour market statistics first releases
Guide to regional and local labour market statistics
How exactly is employment measured?
How exactly is unemployment measured?
Labour force survey (LFS) user guide
Labour force survey quarterly supplement
Labour market assessment
Labour market statistics
Labour market statistics first release historical supplement
Labour market statistics – Northern Ireland
Labour market trends
Measuring low pay
New earnings survey (NES): streamlined analyses (GB)
New earnings survey (NES): analyses by region, county and small areas

New earnings survey (NES): analyses by occupation
New earnings survey (NES): analyses by industry
New earnings survey (NES): analyses for part-time employees; analyses by age group; distribution of hours and of earnings by hours
New earnings survey (NES): analyses by wage negotiating groups: analyses of pension categories
New earnings survey (NES): streamlined analyses (UK)
State of the labour market
What exactly is the labour force survey?

Natural and built environment

Construction statistics annual
Digest of environmental statistics
Drinking water quality in Scotland
Environment in your pocket
Environmental accounts
Environmental protection expenditure by UK industry: a survey of expenditure
Housing statistics annual volume
Housing trends in Scotland
Land use change in England
Municipal waste management survey 2000/01
Operation of the homeless persons legislation in Scotland 1987–88 to 1997–88: national and local authority analyses
Radioactivity in food and the environment
Projections of households in England to 2021
Scottish bathing waters
Scottish household survey
Scottish vacant and derelict land survey
SEPA state of the environment: reports
Sustainable development in the United Kingdom
The environment in your pocket
The Scottish environment statistics

Population and migration

Annual report of the Registrar General for Scotland
Birth statistics: births and patterns of family building, England and Wales
Internal migration

International migration (series MN)
Key population and vital statistics
Longitudinal study 1971–1991: history, organization and quality of data
Marriage, divorce and adoption statistics
Population estimates
National population projections 2000-based
ONS classification of local and health authorities: revised for authorities in 1999
Population projections by ethnic group: a feasibility study
Population projections Scotland (1998 based)
Population trends – quarterly editions
Sub-national population projections

Public sector and other

Electoral statistics
UK defence statistics
UK electoral statistics

Social and welfare

Appeals tribunal quarterly statistics
Carers
Child benefit quarterly statistics
Child Support Agency quarterly statistics
Client group analysis – quarterly bulletins on families with children on key benefits
Client group analysis – quarterly bulletins on the population of working age on key benefits
Client group analysis – quarterly bulletin on the population over state pension age
Disability, care and mobility benefits quarterly statistical enquiry
Family resources survey annual technical report
Family resources survey
Family spending – a report on the 1999–2000 family expenditure survey
Fraud and error in claims for income support and job seekers allowance
Incapacity benefit and severe disablement allowance quarterly statistics
Household satellite account
Households below average income
Housing benefit and council tax benefit annual summary

Housing benefit and council tax benefit quarterly statistics
Industrial injuries disablement benefit quarterly statistics
Internet access
Job seekers allowance quarterly statistics
Living in Britain – General Household Survey
Pensioners' income series
People aged 65 and over
People's perceptions of their neighbourhood and community involvement
Retirement pension statistics
Social focus in brief: children
Social focus in brief: ethnicity
Social focus on men
Social inequalities
Social trends
Tax benefit model tables

Transport, travel and tourism

National travel survey
Overseas travel and tourism
Review of the national travel survey
Road accidents Scotland
Scottish transport statistics
Travel trends – a report on the international passenger survey

US government statistical publications

The US Bureau of Census lists the following information and can be accessed via www.census.gov:

Your gateway to census 2000

Summary file 4 – state by state release summary file 3

People

Estimates
2001 area profiles
Projections
Income

Poverty
International
Genealogy
Housing

Business economic census

Government
E-stats
NAICS
Foreign trade

Geography maps

TIGER
Gazetteer

Newsroom releases

Minority links
Radio/TB
Topics census calendar
The 1930 census
Our centennial
For teachers
American community survey
Statistical abstract
FedStats

Census economic briefing rooms

Monthly trade balance: US international trade in goods and services
Inventories/sales ratios monthly wholesale trade: sales and inventories
Manufacturers' new orders: manufacturers' shipments, inventories, and orders
Value of construction puts in place construction spending
New home sales
Homeownership chart
Durable goods new orders: advance report on durable goods manufacturers' shipments and orders
New housing starts
Total business sales manufacturing and trade inventories and sales

Monthly retail sales advance retail and food service sales

Manufacturing profits per dollar of sales quarterly financial report – manufacturing, mining and trade

Retail profits per dollar of sales quarterly financial report – retail trade

Income by race household income

Poverty rates

Poverty

Reference to any of the above should assist in:

- assessing market shares and identifying the size and growth of existing and new markets;
- identifying trends and how they relate to your own market segment;
- determining the number of customers in a sector;
- determining consumer expenditure in a sector;
- identifying distribution channels;
- determining pricing and price changes;
- estimating world markets, assessing foreign competition and shares of imports and exports overseas.

Most of this information can be obtained from government sources or any large library, or online direct.

BUSINESS LIBRARIES

These are located within the central library in most cities, and should contain the most important reports published by the government. In addition, they usually keep:

- company reports and accounts of the top companies;
- company files containing press cuttings on these companies;
- industry files containing press cuttings on industry sectors;
- official statistics: UK and US Government data, EC, OECD and UN statistics;
- directories, annual year books, standard industry lists and classifications;
- market reports; reports index and research index detailing published market research reports available for purchase.

TRADE ASSOCIATIONS

There are hundreds of associations that represent the interests of particular manufacturers or service providers. Some of these associations also have good library and information facilities. Their main contribution, however, is to be able to provide someone who can answer questions. Their staff have regular contact with the association members and thus have a wealth of market knowledge.

UNIVERSITIES AND COLLEGES

Numerous research projects are completed by graduates and research graduates at universities and colleges. Some of the universities concentrate on various industries and thus have an intimate knowledge of various sectors, and some have departments for marketing their knowledge and research facilities.

INSTITUTES AND PROFESSIONAL ASSOCIATIONS

Organizations such as the Chartered Institute of Marketing and the Market Research Society hold information on industry sectors, markets, products, services, and on consultants and research organizations that can be contacted to obtain further information and help.

USING THE INTERNET TO GATHER INFORMATION

The Internet is being increasingly used to undertake desk research. It is therefore important to understand the opportunity of doing this and how to do it. But the Internet is the 'information highway' and mainly contains information from published material. This material can be referred to for its content and review of companies, markets, customers and potential customers, but review of it has to be defined as a research technique separate from survey research.

The construction of legitimate and professional survey research is a topic on which many books have been written. The use of the Internet as a medium for conducting a survey among users may seem tempting, but unless it is constructed ethically and competently, it will yield misleading results. Amateur research has nothing to commend it, and the use of the Internet in this context also has many complexities, which need to be taken into account. Another book in the Kogan Page Market Research in Practice series will address this.

The strengths and weaknesses of the Internet

Completing desk research via the Internet has both strengths and weaknesses, and understanding this is key to the profitable use of this resource. The Internet is thought by some to be an adventure, and many feel that the most unexpected subjects receive good coverage and equally surprising omissions. This means that it is always worth a quick look, but if you don't find a useful site fairly quickly it may well be more effective to turn to more traditional resources.

The strengths of the Internet are considered to be:

- Access is cheap and information is often free.
- Some subjects are covered in detail.
- There is good background information.
- Information can be obtained quickly.
- There is wide geographic scope.
- There is rapidly increasing coverage.

The weaknesses of the Internet are considered to be:

- Market size figures are not usually available.
- Penetration figures and demographics are not usually available.
- There is a strong US focus.
- There can be patchy coverage.
- Often there is lack of 'authority' in the data.
- Nobody is in control, which causes lack of consistency.
- There are many student and recreational sites with little useful content.

The use of search engines

Search engines are the key to using the Internet for any kind of research. Bookmarks are useful for frequently accessed sites, but spending large amounts of time compiling an extensive collection of bookmarks can be counter-productive. The Internet changes so fast that keeping bookmarks current is a full time task, so it is more sensible to use the resources somebody else has produced.

The following are key sources of information, which can be checked when completing desk research:

Find (Financial Information Net Directory) http://www.find.co.uk

A directory of personal financial services with many appropriate links.

The Search Centre http://www.tka.co.uk/search

Useful information about finding material on the Internet in the business field.

Altavista: http://altavista.com

This is often useful for new subject areas and its coverage is excellent, so it is good for broad searching and for offbeat subjects, but one can be overwhelmed by too many hits. There is a strong US focus, but in the UK it is possible to restrict its search to domain:uk. Altavista allows some structured searching, but search capabilities are still fairly simple compared with online and CD ROM systems. However this search engine allows a more sophisticated search than most of the other engines currently available.

Metaplus: http://www.metaplus.com

Metaplus is a listing or launch pad of sites by subject area.

Excite: http://www.excite.com

Excite allows local searches of UK, French, German or European sites. It is also helpful as it gives a percentage to the relevance ranking.

Northernlight: http://www.northernlight.com

This search engine sets up custom folders, which categorize search results and enable you to refine your search more easily.

Webtop: http://www.webtop.com

This covers Europe and also allows search by individual countries, but it tends to have a very academic bias with virtually no commercial sites included.

Yahoo: http://www.yahoo.com

This is the oldest, much used and still a useful source. It is structured into subject areas, but it also allows keyword searching across categories. As always there is a strong US bias.

http://www.yahoo.co.uk
This is a version of Yahoo which allows searches to be restricted to sites based in UK and Ireland only.

http://gallery.yahoo.com
This part of Yahoo allows searching for images by keyword.

Google: http://www.google.com

The most used search engine in the world today, although it is not particularly good for professional business research.

Hotbot: http://www.hotbot.com

This also gives percentages to the relevance ranking, which can be useful.

Lycos: http://www.lycos.com

It is structured by subject listings, or it is possible to search by a keyword, and it also allows searches for images or sounds.

Easysearcher: http://www.easysearcher.com

It links to over 300 search engines, and it is very useful for the more unusual subjects.

Go: http://www.go.com

This is good for US information. It has wide coverage and also gives percentage relevance rankings.

Ixquick: http://www.ixquick.com

This is a multi search engine, using several other search engines at the same time, using the keywords given.

Dejanews: http://www.dejanews.com

This is useful for searching newsgroups.

Ukindex: http://www.ukindex.co.uk

This lists UK sites and it is not at all comprehensive, but it is a fast way to check if UK information is available.

Britannia: http://www.britannia.com

This is a launch pad for UK sites, and specializes in leisure and recreational information.

Telephone directories

There are business telephone directories available on the Internet and also a smaller selection of residential directories. These are the online equivalent to the *Yellow Pages* or the national telephone books. Some of the most obscure countries are available, but as there are gaps, it is important to check for the specific country required. Some have English versions of the search screen, but many are only in the original language, and the level of searching and ease of use varies considerably. The coverage of the lists below overlaps to a large extent, but they are not identical so it is worth searching around:

http://www.eyp.co.uk

A UK business telephone directory (*Yellow Pages*) searchable by location, subject category or company name. Results are listed alphabetically 10 to a page with a random start letter.

http://www.globalyp.com

This list links to telephone directories, mostly business (*Yellow Pages*) available on the Internet. Coverage is worldwide and some of the most surprising countries are available. Search capabilities are variable, as is English language availability.

http://www.wayp.com

This list links to European telephone directories, mostly business (*Yellow Pages*) available on the Internet. Search capabilities are variable, as is English language availability.

http://www.worldpages.com

This list links to telephone directories, mostly business (*Yellow Pages*) available on the Internet. Coverage is worldwide and some of the most surprising countries are available. Search capabilities are variable, as is English language availability.

http://phonebooth.interocitor.net

This is a world telephone numbering guide to country and area codes, and it offers up-to-date information regarding major telephone numbering system changes worldwide.

Market research data on the Internet

There is not much free market research data on the Internet, but many market research publishers now have Web pages, so the Internet can be a good place for checking the availability of published research. Many will offer free samples from some of their more recent reports. Some important sources are listed below.

Dialog: http://www.dialog.com

Dialog/MAID Profound is a host or supplier rather than a publisher. It therefore offers access to a very wide range of material worldwide, but it has high subscription charges.

Mintel: http://www.mintel.co.uk

Mintel is well known for its published market research reports. It specializes in the UK consumer and retail markets, and this site lists their available reports, with ordering and pricing information.

Euromonitor: http://www.euromonitor.com

Euromonitor is a well established and respected market research publisher. This site lists its available reports, with ordering and pricing information.

Datamonitor: http://www.datamonitor.com

Datamonitor is a well established and respected market research publisher. This site lists its available reports, with ordering and pricing information.

Keynote: http://www.keynote.co.uk

Keynote is a well established and respected market research publisher whose reports cover a wide variety of UK product sectors. This site lists its available reports, with ordering and pricing information.

Romtec: http://www.romtec.co.uk

Publisher of market research in the information technology sector.

Juniper: http://www.jup.com

Juniper Communications is a market research publisher specializing in technology and research about the Internet and online markets.

Killen: http://killen.com

A market research publisher specializing in information technology, banking and financial services, and telecommunications.

Mindbranch: http://www.mindbranch.com

A market research publisher covering a wide range of subject areas including the information technology, Internet, telecommunications, healthcare, financial services and industrial sectors.

Frost and Sullivan: http://www.frost.com

Frost and Sullivan is a very well known company that provides consultancy services and publishes market research. The company covers all the major business-to-business sectors and conducts research in the Asia/Pacific area as well as Europe.

Market Research Society: http://www.mrs.org.uk

The Web site for the Market Research Society.
   www.research-live.com
News and analysis from *Research* magazine, published by the Market Research Society.

ESOMAR: http://www.esomar.nl

The Web site for the European Society for Opinion and Marketing Research (ESOMAR).

Marketing Week: http://www.news-review.co.uk

Marketing Week's online news section.

Business Geographic: http://www.geoweb.co.uk

Business Geographic is a Web site that produces geographic and other cluster analysis based on UK census data, postcode data, Acorn and other sources.

Knauf: http://www.knauffiberglass.com

The home site for a construction company, which gives some very up-to-date market statistics on the construction industry and forecasts.

US Embassy: http://www.usembassy.org.uk

The US Embassy Commercial section in the UK.

Eurostat: http://europa.eu.int

The site of Eurostat, which is the EU's statistical organization.

UK Office for National Statistics: http://www.statistics.gov.uk

Core Web address for the UK Office for National Statistics.

Dun and Bradstreet: http://www.dnb.com

Providers of company information.

Kompass UK: http://www.britishexports.com

Kompass UK company directory.

Thomas Register: http://www.thomasregister.com

This organization lists 155,000 US and Canadian manufacturing companies.

Financial Times Annual Report Service: http://www.annualreports.ft.com

Reports can be ordered free of charge.

The Web is an essential tool for desk research and information development. It is important for finding resources and information, latest practices, for participating in discussions with colleagues and independent experts, and for mentoring opportunities. The rapid pace of change makes the amount of information available online quite bewildering. It is important to search the Internet in a systematic manner and to distinguish between useful information and other information that it is interesting to know. The following is a guide to help managers when completing research.

The first thing to do when searching the Internet is to distinguish between directories. There are two types. Catalogue-style directories are maintained by human editors who index Web pages and reference them under categories that are offered on the screen, such as 'business', 'social sciences', or 'computers'. The best-known example of this type of Web site is currently Yahoo!, at: http://www.yahoo.com. These directories are useful if you are looking for information under a broad heading, such as 'distance learning'. If you are interested in an area covered by one of the categories, this is a good way to begin finding sites on the Web. Each page visited may in turn refer you to other relevant sites.

However, directories will only return search results based on the title and brief descriptions of each site, and they will often only take you to the home page of any site. Therefore they tend to be less effective tools for in-depth content queries.

'Spider-based' search engines are fed by automated 'spider' programs that constantly patrol the Web, indexing URLs and individual pages. Unlike the main directories, they index every significant word of every page, allowing you to enter much more detailed searches. The first few lines or a description of each page are shown on the screen, together with its URL, and if you want to go to that site, you just click on the underlined link.

There are a number of these sites. A favourite is Altavista – it's the fastest, seems to index the most Web sites, and allows the most complex searches. These sites vary widely in the number of pages they index, and the complexity of search criteria they allow. It is well worth trying the same query using several different engines, and comparing the results.

Each search engine has slightly different rules for specifying selection criteria, so it is important to check the instructions for each one. For more complex research you may want to seek professional assistance.

Search tools vary widely in the number of pages they index, and the complexity of search criteria they allow. Again, it is well worth trying the same query using several different engines, and comparing the results. If you are unsure of the timeliness of the Web page that you retrieve, most of the major engines include the date of the pages that they return. If not, your browser may allow you to view some information about the document. This should include the date on which the page was last updated.

Many companies complain that they get too much information from their searches. It is important to think very clearly about exactly what you are looking for, and to put in search criteria that will really narrow down the results. Entering 'distance learning' to Altavista returns 254,698 references. However, adding the term 'software' reduces that to around 600 pages that can then be further broken down. It is also important to search on as many definitions as possible of what you are looking for, as this sometimes provides access to better information. For instance, entering 'consumer reports' will return about 300,000 references. However, adding the terms 'chicken' and 'Eastern Europe' returns just three pages that tell you specifically about Eastern European chicken suppliers.

There are also difficulties in searching on the Internet. These are some common problems and issues:

- **Missing links.** Web sites tend to change very frequently, and you may often encounter referrals to pages that no longer exist, or that no longer contain your search term. The spiders visit each page on an average of once a month, so they cannot be completely up to date at any one time.

   If you think that the site you are looking for should still exist, try clicking into the Location box in your browser, and delete the last section of the URL (after the last /). Then press Enter. This will take you up a level to the referring page, and you may be able to follow the links it contains to find your subject.
- **Domain name not found.** If you get this error, try clicking on the link again immediately. This particular domain name may not have been referenced by anyone before at your Internet provider, and is therefore not in their indexes, which is as far as their server looks on the first request. But if you request the domain a second time, the server will do a lookup beyond its own indexes. Often you will then be able to access the page.
- **Using bookmarks.** Every Web browser should contain a 'bookmark' (or favourite places) function. This allows you to record the URL of the page that you are currently visiting in your own personal directory with one click of the mouse. You can then return to that page later by calling up your bookmarks menu, and clicking

on the name of the page that you wish to revisit. This is useful to keep details of the industry and market sector that relates to your own company, and allows you to update the information regularly.

■ **Using master list sites.** Because the Web changes so much, it is a constant problem to ensure that all your bookmarks are current. Instead of trying to maintain your own exhaustive list of links around a particular subject, check for a master resource site that is updated by a reputable institution such as a library.

■ **Printing and saving information from the Web.** Your browser should allow you to print out any Web page currently on the screen. The command to do this will probably be found in a button on the toolbar, or under the File menu. However, remember that the printed page length will depend on your printer set-up, and may not be exactly as it appears on the screen.

You can also save Web pages to your hard disk for subsequent use in a word processor, spreadsheet or database. Pages can normally be saved either in their tagged HTML version, or in plain text (known as ASCII). This option should be offered to you in the 'Save As' dialog box on your screen. You will probably want to save documents as ASCII text unless you are studying HTML, and specifically wish to see the source code for a particular page.

Remember that you will only save the text of the page by using the File menu 'Save As' command. Images that you see within the Web page actually come from separate files. However, many browsers will also allow you to capture these graphics files. In Netscape for Windows this is done by pointing to the graphic and clicking on the right mouse button. Check your own browser manual for specific instructions.

■ **Copyright issues.** Much of the information that is available on the Web is in the public domain – that is, free to be used by you after you download it. However, if you see a copyright notice you should certainly respect it. And if you are intending to quote someone, it is courteous to request their permission first – use the e-mail address given on the Web page.

Using mailing lists and newsgroups

Many people forget that there is more to the Internet than the World Wide Web. It is beneficial to explore electronic discussion lists and newsgroups. These exist for a diverse list of subjects, of both professional and recreational interest. Subscribing to them can give you access to a group of worldwide experts that you probably could not find by any other means. Of course, as with all forms of research, you need to exercise your own judgement as to the quality of information – there are also many people masquerading as experts!

The main difference between discussion lists and newsgroups is that messages posted to an electronic mailing list automatically come to your online in-box every time you collect your e-mail. An active list will generate a good deal of traffic, and your in-box can quickly overflow. If you decide to subscribe to one of these groups, check whether it has a 'digest' version. This sends out messages in batches under a contents list that can be quickly scanned for items of interest, and then deleted.

A newsgroup is essentially a bulletin board, which you have to remember to check for new postings. Most Web browsers now incorporate a newsgroup reader. If yours does not, your Internet provider should be able to supply you with one of the freely available programs.

Often there are both a list and a newsgroup devoted to the same, or similar, subjects. Whichever you decide to use will depend on whether you like to have the material from the mailing lists, or whether you would rather leave your mailbox clear, and search the newsgroups when you are ready. It is possible to do both.

Finding mailing lists or newsgroups

You can search for mailing lists and newsgroups on particular subjects by using one of two World Wide Web sites: http://www.liszt.com gives you a searchable directory of e-mail discussion groups, and http://www.dejanews.com will refer you to the Deja News Research Service that allows you to search for newsgroups. For both of these sites, you supply your subject of interest. The sites will then return a list of relevant mailing groups, with instructions on how to subscribe or obtain further information on each one, or a list of newsgroups with recent postings on your topic.

Some of the search engines can also be set to look for newsgroup postings that contain your keywords. In Altavista, this is done by changing the Search box from 'the Web' to 'Usenet'. Scanning the results of your inquiry will give you a good idea of newsgroups that might be useful to you.

If you join one of these discussions, you need to follow some basic rules, known as 'Netiquette', which tell you how to behave on the Net. The most important of these is to ask specific questions. If you ask a question, make it easy for people to reply. Queries such as 'Does anyone know anything about widgets?' are unlikely to attract any (polite) answers. Make your posting short, and very clear as to what you need.

Commercial services

Commercial services such as America Online can also be great sources for research, if they have forums that meet your needs. America Online has a wealth of information about any location or subject, both recreational and business-oriented. Both services also offer resources and forums where members can discuss issues relating to small and home-based businesses. They provide listings of, and clickable links to, Web sites for categories such as company and stock research.

SURVEY RESEARCH

Once Internet searches are completed, data collected and other desk research completed, analysed and interpreted, a manager can start to think about adding to the information by designing survey research. It is important at this point to refer to the list prepared earlier, 'What data do I need?' and develop a list of issues to research. This will help in designing the survey and questionnaire. These issues can be evaluated in the following ways.

Using qualitative information

Many companies are satisfied with using quantitative information, as it gives them independent facts and data on the market. It gives enough information to plan marketing and monitor its effectiveness. However, it will not give the reasons behind the facts, or more importantly, the attitudes of the current and potential market to the company's products or services. Qualitative information provides this key additional input to decision making, or provides information on the 'language' of the consumer, key reasons for using the products and what are the key marketing factors.

Using quantitative information

Evaluating marketing objectives

The essential marketing information to set the marketing objectives and to be able to appraise and review them on a regular basis is:

- sales statistics analysed on a quarterly and annual basis;
- market share information by geographical and business market;
- financial performance both quarterly and annually.

Assessing marketing strategies

As we shall see later in the book, marketing strategies can be set if the company has regular survey information tracking products, defining trends in markets and evaluating product performance in a competitive tracking analysis. But at this stage it is important to know the options for the different types of research studies that can be developed.

Tracking marketing tactics

This type of survey monitors the effectiveness of marketing tactics by tracking advertising awareness and recall, responses to other promotions, and buyers' attitudes to all sales methods used.

Evaluating marketing objectives

Marketing objectives can be set effectively if the reasons behind the trends in the market are understood. Understanding why there is a market potential and what are the competitive reasons for market share help a company to define the marketing objectives and the task to increase sales to improve company profitability.

In setting marketing strategies a manager needs a clear understanding of the options offered by each strategy, and the likely results of choosing one option in preference to another. Researching the competitive positioning in the market by determining penetration in the market will help to define a market penetration strategy, to enter more of the market and increase market share.

Assessing marketing objectives

If a marketing objective has been to find new markets to enter, research can assist by evaluating the reasons that new customers might buy the company's products or services. Equally, if markets are to be segmented effectively into different types of customer, each with different needs, then a new market opportunity might be identified as a potential opportunity in one of the segments.

Research into the reasons that a product is or is not liked by consumers can help to define new product improvements and thus a new product opportunity. Marketing strategies for new product opportunities can also be evaluated if new product ideas, product concepts, product prototypes and test products are given to current and potential customers to test out. Usually an existing product is paired with a product concept, and consumers are asked to test out each one and say which they prefer. This is more commonly known as a paired comparison test. Sometimes one concept is tested against another concept to see which is preferred. This helps a company to prioritize product opportunities or, in some instances, eliminate options that are unattractive to customers.

Research is vital in strategic evaluation if new ideas for diversifying the business are evaluated or tested out. A company entering a new market with a new product is unlikely to know much about that market, and is going to be dependent on good information for decision making for developing sales of the new product and services. The research is likely to reduce the uncertainty about pursuing the diversification opportunity, and to help managers to plan, based on known and defined customer needs.

EVALUATING MARKETING TACTICS

Research techniques in the 1990s were developed by managers to evaluate marketing tactics and now, in the new century, this aspect of market research is being used effectively. Qualitative evaluation of tactics has a direct effect on how these tactics are developed and used to increase sales.

Good evaluation qualitatively, to establish customers' attitudes and motivations towards the way a company organizes its marketing tactics, can be used in the quantitative surveys designed to track marketing tactics. Usually this is done through the development of 'attitude' statements in the qualitative research and then applying the statements to the target customers by getting them to agree or disagree with them when assessing the marketing methods. The statements must reflect the 'language' of the customer, which is particularly important when you complete global market research.

There are three different types of marketing tactic that can be assessed effectively through market research.

Attitude to products

Research into attitudes and motivations towards products helps managers to understand the consumer 'terminology' towards the products. In effect it is the way in which consumers describe a product, the language they use, that can be used to promote the product to other consumers. Consumer descriptions of a product such as 'easy to bite', 'appetising' and 'healthy' are ways in which a product can be assessed, and indicate consumers' likes and dislikes for it.

In the sausage market international differences show how language is important. Consumers in the UK are more interested in a 'nourishing' breakfast with a cooked breakfast sausage, while in Australia consumers buy sausages for the 'barbie' (barbecue).

Assessment of prices

Qualitative research helps managers to understand price acceptability and the way in which a consumer evaluates and measures prices. Actual price paid compared with value for money needs to be assessed to understand consumers' attitudes to the purchase. Once this has been done consumers are also receptive to discussing how price changes can affect their purchase decisions. Often price is less important than other product details.

Evaluation of advertising and promotions

Communications concept evaluation and acceptance is the most applied use of qualitative techniques. Many advertising agencies use the technique to prove or disprove the creative ideas that they have developed for advertising campaigns. One limitation of this approach is that it can confirm ideas that may not relate totally to customers' needs and particular types of customer in a market. It is likely also to focus on short-term requirements for a product and not to concentrate on the fundamental needs and purchase decisions taken by a consumer when buying a product.

A more effective use of qualitative techniques for communications development and evaluation is to use the research to:

- Identify which features of the product or service the consumers are aware of and associate with.
- Determine what benefits of the product or service are realized and appreciated by consumers.
- Test out themes and concepts, which communicate the benefits to the potential customers, the features of which are highlighted in the advertising. Benefits are most successfully evaluated with 'slogans' or 'strap lines', which in an amusing or direct manner tell the customer why he or she will benefit from buying the product. These also should be tested out for their suitability and fit with customers, to ensure that copy in communications is worded in a way that consumers understand.

CASE STUDY

A private bank: using information to target customers

Private banks have traditionally found their customers by having them referred by other very satisfied customers. This means that their main contact with customers is not through the disciplines and techniques of sales and marketing, but primarily through high quality customer service. At the start of the 1990s the financial markets and the financial services sector became very competitive, with many companies offering similar facilities and services and moving 'up market' to develop the personal banking sector. It has therefore been difficult for financial services organizations to find more of their traditional type of customer, let alone expand their base to attract new types of customers who might have become more attracted to, or more eligible for, their services.

This private bank recognized that it could not develop a sales and marketing plan without good information to give it direction on how to promote and market its services. But what did it know about its customers, and how could this understanding of the customer base help to find new customers?

The unfortunate fact was that it did not have any data with which it could carry out a systematic analysis of the customer base and the potential market. There was no desk research that could provide a cost effective answer, so to get the information it really needed it had to develop a system for setting up customer analysis and customer satisfaction assessment.

The private bank had developed a customer records system, which collected many personal details about customers, and aided the organization in providing its high quality customer service. However few managers took care in filling in the details and updating the records, and those who did so only carried out the task with little detail as a formality, to record the last customer contact, rather than to make a contribution to the development of the sales and marketing system by providing marketing information.

The extent of the data collected about a customer is seen in Table 2.3, which is an extract of the computer output from a customer record card. It can be seen from this that there is more than enough information to develop an overall analysis of the present customer base. This might then highlight certain characteristics that could be used in deciding to whom to promote the service.

Table 2.3 *Bank internal information system*

Name	Type
First:	Status:
Family name:	Security:
	Priority:
	Net worth:
	Income:
Business name:	A/C Executive Officer:
Occupation:	
Family name:	Introduced by:
Occupation:	Manner of introduction:
Nationality:	Prospect for further:
	Introduction:

Table 2.3 *Continued*

Birth date:	
Last contact:	Result:
Next call:	Result:
Achieved:	
Planned:	
Home address:	Phone:
	Fax:
Postcode:	Telex:
Location:	E-mail:
ACORN area:	
Business address:	Phone:
	Fax:
Postcode:	Telex:
Location:	E-mail:

Analysis of the data would:
- define the characteristics of the present customer by:
    - age;
    - income;
    - occupation;
    - length of time a customer;
    - volume of personal capital;
    - likely inheritance;
- establish the concentration of the customer base geographically;
- identify who referred them to the private bank, to establish whether there is any particular type of person who tends to refer people: friends, professional advisors, etc.

The result of this analysis gave the private bank sufficient information to decide who to target:

■ high income earners in professions – accountants, solicitors, barristers, management consultants, landowners and property developers;

■ people who live in certain postcode areas (defined later in the book as geodemographic areas 34 and 36 of the Acorn analysis);

■ the 35–54 age group who are in the mid and late family lifestages;

■ those who also want to use their investments as collateral for other financial ventures;

■ those interested in offshore funds.

This profile therefore enabled the sales staff, for the first time, to isolate the particular type of person who was a potential customer.

The bank also decided to carry out a survey among customers to establish what benefits they felt were provided by being a customer. But they were nervous of the procedure of approaching the customer in this manner, because of the personal nature of this banking service. However a list of contacts was agreed and without much problem in getting cooperation, in-depth interviews were completed with both private and commercial customers. What was interesting was the degree to which the style of customer service influenced the customers' attitudes towards the private bank. It was not just that it was perceived to be better than other banks; it was the fact that the bank delivered good customer service consistently that was important to the customer. The findings of the survey were input into the marketing information system and used to monitor the consistency and quality of customer service standards.

The result of this initiative was to use geodemographic data in the areas of the country identified with a high concentration of potential customers, and to develop a telephone marketing campaign backed by personal visits to promote personal service banking. Telephone calls were introduced to talk to potential customers about why the bank felt they would be 'ideal' customers. Brochures were also developed which featured the importance of consistent customer service. The campaign was launched at a time when bank services were being scrutinized by high value consumers, so the timing had good results in attracting customers who met the criteria of the bank's customer profile.

CASE STUDY

Book jackets: analysing a sales problem

Marketing communications are also key at the point of sale in retail sales. One of the most interesting examples of how promotions need to be researched is a case study which was published in the Market Research Society journal *Survey* about Agatha Christie books.

In 1985 the publisher HarperCollins found sales were declining, but was uncertain about the reasons for this decline. A research company carried out a mix of desk research, qualitative and quantitative research to understand the underlying trends in the market and specific reasons for the drop in sales.

The desk research showed that the number of adults claiming to have bought a paperback in the previous 12 months had declined from 20.9 million to 19.6 million – which was around 1 per cent a year. The market was biased towards the young, those in the higher socio-economic groups and the better educated. But this data was not convincing enough to clarify why the sales were declining, so a list of issues to be evaluated was developed and agreed.

The next stage of the research was qualitative, through four group discussions with current readers of Agatha Christie books and buyers of general paperbacks. Groups of 15–24-year-olds and 35–44-year-olds were recruited. The groups were mixed in terms of sex, and two of the four groups were the ABCI socio-economic grade; the other two were C2D grades. The purpose of the groups was to discover how the book readers viewed crime in relation to other genres. They also had to assess Christie and how her style of writing compared with other writers. The group respondents also were shown the different cover designs, which over 20 years had changed significantly, and invited to comment on them. More group discussions were also carried out with 'non-readers', those who had seen Christie films or read other crime books, but not actually read the Christie books.

The findings of the groups confirmed that there was interest in crime writing, with Christie being viewed as the 'queen of crime'. Christie crimes were perceived to provide 'active reading', the murders in her books were described as always 'nice', and her style invited 'participation'. Most of the books feature Hercule Poirot or Miss Marple, and it was these characters rather than the author that appeared to deter people from buying books. With Christie visual presentation was also found to be important.

The groups also found that the book jackets on the books at the time of the research did not convey the qualities of the author. They featured 'blood and gore', following a trend in the book market, which had seen a rise in the sales of horror books. The research showed that the Christie readers turned away from the gory aspects of crime, not being totally interested in the details. It was the horror-style covers that were causing the sales to decline. In fact in most of the Christie stories the actual murder is not described, but a victim or murder weapon is found and the actual murder is left to the reader's imagination without any detailed description.

HarperCollins produced a sales pack for representatives to use when calling on their main customers, the bookshop chains, providing all the details of the research. In addition a sales campaign was launched and totally new book covers were created. The research had been effective in finding the problem, so the publisher used the research effectively.

After the campaign four more group discussions were completed to identify if readers had noticed any differences. The new jacket designs were perceived to be seen as 'intriguing' and 'subtle'. They were thought to be 'suitable for nice murders'. The pictures on the jacket were seen to link with the title, and the design conveyed quality. The new theme for the covers was developed into point-of-sale promotions and advertising.

As a result of this research sales of Agatha Christie paperbacks increased by 40 per cent in the first year – 1 million units increasing to 1.4 million units.

This case study shows the importance of checking with potential buyers before considering any changes in presentation or the style of covers, which need to communicate the content of the book. It also shows that marketing benefits can be obtained from research very quickly after the research has been completed.

Research helps managers to understand what consumers consider to be the unique selling points (USPs) of a product or service. Once identified, they can be incorporated in the marketing communications and tested out by researching concepts. If USPs are targeted well, current and potential customers will relate to them and confirm through research that they will be effective in marketing the product.

DEVELOPING TREND INFORMATION

Many companies are now more used to referring to customer profile information because of database packages marketed with computer systems software. There is an increased need to ensure that potential customers can be located cost effectively. Getting the information you really need from these databases depends on manipulating the output of the data from the computer to get it to tell a story.

Referring to the data on a monthly basis and comparing the analysis of that month with the same period in the previous year, two years, three years or more is just a 'snapshot'. This picture only informs a manager that he/she is doing better or worse than before, and it does not give sufficient indication about the action he/she should take.

If this data is analysed in either tabular or graphic format over a longer time period, say at least three years, then trends can start to be identified and it makes the information meaningful. At a glance a manager can see the pattern of the statistics – increasing, remaining static or declining – and without any further difficulty can start to make decisions about the appropriate actions. This method is also effective from the point of view of keeping the volume of data manageable and ensuring that those who are not used to being analytical can start to use data for good decision making.

Later in the book we will be discussing the most effective techniques in survey research for assisting managers to use data to increase sales. The principle of trend information in these surveys applies in the same way as for internal information. However, there are important techniques to review for these surveys. The most important aspect to appreciate is that effective and actionable survey information can only be collected if surveys are carried out over a series of time periods, plotting trends and monitoring needs of customers.

TARGETING THROUGH DATABASE MARKETING

The increasing use of computers has caused the development of database marketing, which includes the growth of lifestyle databases and geodemographics. Linked with this, the growing activities of database marketing have encouraged institutions to develop customer databases. In financial institutions this has required a change of focus from account-based computer systems to customer-based databases. And in recent years the Internet has set new challenges.

All of this will grow further in the future as firms and institutions become totally computer dependent and managers develop further their analytical skills to aid decision making. In association with this:

- Geodemographics will provide further customer data, to be linked with internal information as the classification systems become meaningful in relation to account usage, policy purchase or investment decision making.
- Developments in both hardware or software will provide the window of opportunity for managers to improve their skills.
- Geographic information systems, digital mapping-based databases will provide companies with even more focused abilities to target customers in a more localized way and plot demand geographically.
- Internet analysis software or Web site user software will help to define whom the organization is communicating with.

This also means that management will become more sophisticated in its needs for information, and internal and external data will integrate into the marketing information system and the company's management information system. The result will be the reality that the MIS is the focal point for strategy development and monitoring sales, marketing and communications methods.

HINTS ABOUT GETTING THE INFORMATION YOU REALLY NEED

- It is important for managers to realize that the company needs to develop an 'information culture' and become analytical in its approach to decision making.

- Defining what data is needed internally and externally establishes essential data.
- Develop a marketing information system, but 'customize' it to the company, its product range and the markets in which it operates.
- Present internal data in a format that is easy to interpret, preferably graphic.
- Check out what desk research exists to give background information.
- Decide what survey data is needed and plan it in a series of research phases designed to provide trend information related to the buying habits and needs of customers.
- Hold a series of management workshops to discuss how the information should be used.
- Generate data, which helps in planning and monitoring marketing objectives, marketing strategies and marketing tactics.
- Define which target audience to communicate with and research.
- Identify what communications need to be evaluated.
- Decide how to measure the results of the communications.

3 The best research techniques anyone can use

INTRODUCTION

Market research has two important functions for managers. They are to reduce any uncertainty that managers might have in taking decisions, by giving them intelligence, data, statistics and information on which to base the rationale for the decisions they take; and to enable managers to monitor the sales and marketing decisions that have been taken, to identify whether they were right, whether they need to be revised and whether they need total rethinking.

Using market research to increase sales depends on developing a systematic market research programme, customized for a company and integrated into the management planning system. The key to using this research programme effectively is to do the following:

- Develop a sales, marketing and communications strategy with detailed actions for its implementation.
- Develop a series of ideas that can be evaluated through research, and proved or disproved as to whether they would help to develop the strategy.

■ Develop a database on the size, shape and nature of a market and its structure, to understand the environment in which the managers are taking their decisions.

■ Assess the acceptability of the company's products in the market and the understanding of the advertising and promotions in the potential customer base, in order to target sales, marketing and communications effectively.

■ Analyse the research to ensure that it can be acted on and is not just information to refer to.

If this is completed by any company then the management team will have sufficient data to decide on the actions it can take after the research. Further research would assess the success of these actions and identify what other actions are important to take. Managers therefore can use research findings to improve the ways in which sales, marketing and communications methods are organized by the company. This whole process helps to develop a company's products and communications in such a way that they correspond to the buying behaviour of customers and potential customers.

The difficulty with market research is that it is complex, and involves using statistical and analytical techniques, which, if used incorrectly, may not provide usable information. Those who use research techniques that were not planned well may find that the information provided by the research is difficult to action. This information might be correct as a series of facts, but often managers find that the research is not of use to them, as they cannot decide what actions to take as a result of reading the data. It may also not help to identify a trend.

The best techniques that any manager can use depend on the research being developed, planned and implemented effectively. In planning, the more time that is taken in discussing how the research will be carried out, the better the research will be. This applies to developing the issues to be researched and also particularly to the format of a questionnaire, since reviewing its structure, agreeing the phraseology of the questions and thinking about how the results of the research will be used will have a direct influence on the quality of the research. In its implementation, the longer the time the project takes, the better the quality of the result, as the interviewing will have been done carefully, the analysis of the data completed with precision and the interpretation of the results reasoned in the context of market trends or customer needs. A well planned research project is likely to be implemented well, since the results of the research will be clear to managers and the answers to the questions will provide immediate direction, allowing decisions to be taken. A manager cannot go wrong if he or she proceeds in a definite pattern in planning and carrying out research.

Before any survey research is carried out, it is important to establish whether any published data would solve the sales, marketing or communications problem or help to take the right decisions. Any survey that is designed by a manager is not likely to be planned well unless the manager can understand the emphasis or positioning of the company or its products in the market. Brand share data would help in this respect, but it needs to be linked with a trend analysis to understand the performance of the company or its products in the market. Once these issues have been evaluated and developed then a manager will have the rationale for designing a specific survey. Having referred to published and brand share data, the manager is more likely to design a better survey, as the research will have taken account of the key issues in the market.

A marketing director the author has worked with has said of research:

> A blind man uses a white stick to avoid walking into large obstacles in his path and to define his passage around the world. Market research is the businessman's white stick. It prevents him from blundering sightlessly into large objects designed to do his company significant financial damage.

COLLECTING PUBLISHED DATA

Any manager, budget conscious and cautious of developing an information system that does not contain the right information, will want to collect existing published information before commissioning special projects. Data may already exist which answers a marketing, communications or sales problem, or provides a further insight into a situation and helps in designing the analysis needed to solve the problem. The best technique to use when exploring published information is to follow a procedure which gives reassurance that all possible sources of information are explored, evaluated and if necessary eliminated.

First, check the information that exists in your own company. Past managers may have carried out some research and the findings of it, although possibly out of date, may provide an indication of the issues related to the problem or market analysis being considered. Also try to develop a 'centre of excellence' for all this published data, such as a library or information unit. If there is published data already in the company, it must be accessible by all levels of management. I was once completing a survey for a company and at one of the review meetings a senior manager said he had found a report that gave an account of a similar project, but it was 10 years out of date. When I explained to the manager that it would be useful as it provided benchmark data against which the new data could be compared, he apologized for not bringing it from his home earlier in the discussions. This manager did not realize the importance of keeping that data in the office in a central information system.

Many companies are recognizing the investment in information that they are making, and are using the resources of new technology to provide an effective internal database on published information. An example of this is a multinational financial services company that runs a central information facility on its computer, which is accessible by any manager in any of its offices worldwide. Any internal or externally commissioned project is recorded in this system by means of a short summary that shows:

- the country in which the research is carried out;
- the target market researched;
- the objectives of the research project;
- the research method used;
- the key findings of the research and important data that is regularly monitored in all research projects to update trend analyses;
- whether the data in the research was within the known norms of the market, and if it was different from the norm, how different it was;
- whether respondents in the survey were asked if they would participate in future research;
- the implications of the research and which managers need to take actions as a result;
- the actions taken, and any issues learnt as a result, which are helpful in ensuring that the project is improved if commissioned again at a later date.

Users in this organization are pleased with the system. They say that using the data is helpful because data can be accessed quickly, the data gives an insight into an issue or problem at the time it is being discussed at a touch of a button, and it helps to ensure that future research is planned better and more effectively.

If internal data does not assist, the next phase is to refer to external information. Business libraries, online search systems, universities, research institutes and trade associations are all key sources of information.

There is also an excellent directory called *Market Search* (Arlington Publications), which is a complete listing of research in most product categories. Under each category heading are listed all the published reports on that category worldwide. Each entry provides the title of the report, a brief synopsis of the report, the number of pages, the publisher and the price. The entries are coded by the publishing company, and cross-referencing the code with the list of companies at the back of the book yields the name, address, telephone and fax numbers of each company. More details about the reports and ordering information can be obtained from the companies listed.

Even if you cannot find the data you need through an exhaustive evaluation of published data, contact with all possible data sources allows your name to be put on mailing lists, and updates can be sent to you which may help you identify useful new data.

USING BRAND SHARE DATA

Many industries only use sales statistics as a basis on which to measure sector performance, product performance and competitor activity. Government data and manufacturers' sales data is often collected, analysed and disseminated by trade and industry associations on behalf of the industry and members of these associations. This is an effective way of understanding:

- the size of the market;
- trends in the market;
- who the market leaders are;
- which market segments and product sectors are performing well;
- domestic versus overseas business segments;
- legal and regulatory issues that relate to the market.

In some sectors, such as the insurance sector, the pharmaceutical sector, the tyre sector and the automotive sector, manufacturers and service providers supply their sales data to an independent objective analysis company. The data is entered into a computer and an analysis developed. Each participant to the brand share data exchange gets the following data:

- information on the size of the market;
- its own sales in relation to the total sales in the market;
- its brand shares by each product category;
- its sales by main distributors and retailers.

This data is very useful for developing competitive product strategies, setting objectives of increasing market share, and identifying where certain product sectors need regenerating and developing.

We will see later in the book how monitoring market shares become important for tracking trends in markets. Some sectors have developed procedures for brand share monitoring. These include the following.

A retail audit or consumer panel which is used to monitor brand shares

A retail audit is based on selecting a sample of retail stores, which are representative of the volume of business transacted through all outlets. A retail audit is very useful as, apart from providing the method for recording the sales and brand shares, it can be used as a mechanism for assessing the product penetration and distribution achieved.

A consumer panel is set up by recruiting a group of private households and interviewing a member of the household. The consumer panel can be used to develop information about the types of consumer responding to the products, product purchase, whether they are likely to buy the product, and how much they are prepared to pay for the product.

Predictive models

These are usually set up by analysing three types of data:

- penetration data: the proportion of buyers in the population who purchase a product;

- repeat purchase data: the proportion of buyers in the population who purchase a product more than once;
- buying rates factor: a weighting factor that is added to the analysis to assess whether the buying process is an average purchase or not.

DEVELOPING CUSTOMER DATA

Good managers are analytical, ready to question their decisions and receptive to testing out ideas and using information to influence their decisions. However, the type of data we have reviewed so far is not likely to help good managers to achieve this ideal situation, as the data collected is unlikely to be sufficiently specific or relevant to the decisions that need to be taken. It is therefore essential and interesting to managers to be able to create, design and initiate their own tailor-made surveys to help them approach their sales, marketing and communications decisions with information-based confidence.

However, the process of developing customer data is a complex procedure of initiating a company culture that is receptive to using information, and also deciding on, developing, modifying and running systems that relate to the whole process of satisfying the company's present and potential customers. The cultural development also relates to management procedures in the short and long term, and how the data becomes integrated into the company and its management procedures.

In the short term, it is a matter of seeing what data is already available, as reviewed earlier in this chapter. It is also important to review a number of factors to agree what customer data is needed. Management has to establish what assumptions it has taken, and decide how it has to understand the market and customer needs more clearly. It also has objectively to come to terms with recognizing that it has to decide what new information it ought to use to learn about its customers. The third and the most challenging action it has to take is to think about what customers might or might not like, new product or communications ideas, and hypotheses about how customers might react to new approaches or ideas considered by the company. As many companies do not use research in this way, it is important to change the whole philosophy of the company.

In the longer term, the management team has to decide what regular information is needed about customers, to identify any trends that might emerge in the market. It also has to understand customers' attitudes and how they change, their behaviour and how it can be influenced, and how certain segments of the market become regular or loyal customers for specific reasons. The most effective customer databases can also provide an early warning system to establish if customers' attitudes or behaviour is changing, and if competitor activity causes changes or differences in market activity.

The key to developing customer data that becomes effective information for increasing sales is to classify the customer base, using definitions that characterize the customer in the marketplace. Consumer markets are generally classified by defining consumers according to their age, sex and social class (or income) and increasingly geodemographic analyses, depending on which consumer classification system is used.

Industrial markets are classified by the type of organization in the context of its international industrial classification, the size of the company in terms of its sales, number of employees and whether it is a new company, developing company or well established in its particular segment.

The interesting fact about these classification systems is that they are unlikely to help to increase sales. They are more likely to tell you about your customers, who they are, where they are, what they want, what they like or dislike. For industrial customers it will tell you who they are, where they are and what they like or dislike, but it will also establish how they buy, why they buy and who should be influenced in the buying process.

Managers who become more experienced in developing customer data have been able to improve on the standard classification systems and develop customer characterizations that are more relevant and more appropriate for their businesses. This includes classifying individuals by their various contacts – customers, potential customers and other – as well as identifying whether they have knowledge of your company and its product and services.

Customers need to be classified as:

■ current customers, who need to be assessed as to how satisfied they are with your products and services;
■ potential customers, who need to be persuaded to use your products and services;
■ owners and users, who need to be monitored for their usage of the products to establish whether the product benefits were delivered and when they will buy again;

■ buyers, who may not be the users but who have a clear attitude towards the competitive positioning of the products and services, having taken a decision to buy your product in preference to competitors' products;

■ particularly in industrial markets, intermediaries or influencers who may give advice or recommendations to customers on which products to buy.

In the 1980s a whole new industry grew up based on the use of geodemographics. These organizations have developed census-based geodemographics, lifestyle and credit-based data into marketing information resources. A benefit of using these systems is that they can be customized on your company's computer system. This will be discussed in more detail in the next chapter.

CASE STUDY

Map, atlas and travel guide publishers: using research techniques to monitor the market

The publishing sector has only become oriented to using research in the last 20 years. It traditionally used sales data as a basis for customer monitoring and defining market share, so it was missing an opportunity for effective branding and targeting to its customers. At that time map, atlas and travel guide publishers perceived their customers as bookstores – retailers – rather than the end-buyers, users and readers of its products. They carried out no market analysis to define the characteristics of current and potential customers, and therefore could not give help to bookstores in promoting and selling their guides to the most likely potential customers. They also had no information about trends in the market, which could have helped them to allocate and set product development and promotional budgets to capitalize on changing customer needs, and to monitor competitor activity.

A group of US map, atlas and travel guide publishers decided to collaborate to develop a research group in 1991, to provide cost effective research. In this way an individual publisher could share industry data, but analyze it in ways that related to its own specific needs. Two specific studies were set up annually which have become central to the publishers' sales, marketing and communications planning.

First, an annual store survey was developed, to monitor sales, marketing and communications with the publishers' immediate customers, bookshops. Rather than just confirming what publishers already knew about their retailers, the survey asked bookstores to provide feedback on the sales, marketing and communications support provided by publishers. The benefit of this to the publishers using this data has been that they are encouraged to evaluate the nature of their support while comparing it with that of their competitors. In addition, over a period of years, they are able to monitor whether the support they are providing is consistent, and if changes need to be made, where budget allocations can be provided. The survey has also helped independent map stores in the United States to define the product profile they need to maintain in order to compete with retail chain stores.

Second, a consumer contact and household survey was also set up to define the users and buyers, non-users and non-buyers of each of the product categories. This survey assessed which products individuals bought, where they bought them, awareness of publishers and their marketing, their travel patterns, and use and purchase of the products when travelling. The survey has helped to define market segments, identify opportunities for product development, and monitor promotions.

The benefit of these surveys to the publishers has been to provide a profile of the present and potential customer base, and enable them to decide which targets to concentrate on to increase their sales. In addition, the trend analysis has allowed the publishers to view product development and market development in a more systematic and structured manner. Prior to using the data, most of the publishers viewed the products as one overall category – maps, atlases and guides – only distinguishing between them when a new series or title launch was developed. The consumer survey trends showed that the profile and buying habits of consumers for each product category were different, implying that marketing methods needed to be applied to each as a segment in its own right. The map segment had a broad socio-economic profile, but purchase was concentrated in the 25–34 age group and it was primarily a male market. The atlas segment was also broad in socio-economic profile, but purchase and use spread from under 18 up to 55 plus, for schools and the gift market. The travel guide segment is a defined market, mainly upmarket, with buyers in the 35–44 age group and primarily female. The result of this analysis was a complete change in management decision making towards each segment of the market, for cost effective targeting.

One of the most important developments of this research was to relate the data to lifestyle information. Questions were added to the questionnaire asking consumers to classify themselves as follows:

- an 'Active City Visitor' – keen on seeing the sights, going to exhibitions and so on;
- a 'Non-active City Visitor' – the shopper and person looking for a place to eat or drink, or just needing street information;
- an 'Outdoor Recreationer' – a hiker, walker, camper or the like;
- a 'Family Sightseer' – driving to national parks and recreation areas;
- a 'Foreign Traveller' – who travels outside the United States.

This additional lifestyle analysis has given the publishers the opportunity of analysing the information in the context of the habits and preferences of consumers. Relating this to the products that they have bought in the past and those they are interested in buying in the future, it provided more specific information for understanding the use of maps, atlases and travel guides.

As the studies have progressed over the last 10 years the trend data has been used to identify, measure and quantify market shares. This has assisted with sales and communications programme resource allocation and planning. The studies have therefore used traditional techniques to provide a whole industry with information on how it performs.

CUSTOMIZING RESEARCH TECHNIQUES

The approach shown in the case study above is not unusual to a number of industry sectors, especially the food, drink, travel and financial services sectors. The surveys described are essentially industry surveys, providing the background to the market, the performance in the industry and the key trends that exist. Companies in these industries have learnt to use the profile of the consumers in the database, the incidence of buyers and non-buyers and the awareness of the companies and their brand in the sector to develop customized databases. Other surveys exist, but they tend only to monitor sales via major accounts.

Generally there are two types of survey that provide specific data for these companies. They are as follows.

User and attitude surveys, usually known as 'U & A'

These tend to be surveys among product users, relating the profile of these consumers to 'attitude' statements, which are used to describe what they like or dislike about the products.

Awareness and attitude surveys

These are surveys that monitor competitive awareness of brands and manufacturers, also linking them with 'attitude statements' used to describe what customers like or dislike about the products. However, it is only after these surveys have been run at least twice that these databases become effective. When used in conjunction with the general industry surveys, marketing information can be used to relate to specific management and marketing issues. We will see in the next chapter how a customizing measurement technique achieves this.

KNOWING THE MARKET UNIVERSE

An important aspect in developing the surveys is to make them as representative of the market as possible. A full census is prohibitive to complete, as the cost and logistics of doing this are beyond the resources of any organization. Sample surveys are the norm, and if planned well their results can be representative of the full population within plus or minus 5 per cent confidence limits, giving as accurate information as possible.

There are differences between techniques for knowing the market in consumer and business-to-business research, and it is important to be clear about the application of basic sampling techniques, to give management the confidence that their data is 'robust'.

Taking the example of the US map, atlas and travel guide survey, the sampling for this consumer survey is completed as follows. The US Bureau of Census gives the demographic profile of the US population in age, income and location by state, urban, suburban and rural areas. There are some 48 cities in the United States that have a good cross-section of population, and shopping malls and strip malls where research can be carried out. Interviewing in these areas gives market researchers a high chance of getting a full quota of respondents, and so the survey is designed by allocating a quota for each of the cities that are selected for the interviews. The interviewer selects respondents by classifying them by age and income, and only interviews those who qualify, making the sample interviewed representative of the US population by matching the defined quota.

The interviewer then asks the respondents, 'Have you bought a map, atlas or travel guide in the last 12 months?' This information allows the interviewer to allocate the respondent to the category of 'buyer' or 'non-buyer'. The survey then continues with questions about the products individual respondents buy, the stores they buy in, their use of the Internet, their recreational activities and so on. The survey is therefore representative of the market, and testing of the data by statisticians shows that the data is in fact representative to within plus or minus 3 per cent accuracy, which makes it a very effective market monitor.

In business to business research the proper process is very different, and in our experience it is not carried out by as many organizations as it should be, as organizations tend to believe interviewing a sample of their customers will provide sufficient representation. Take for example an international publisher of legal and regulatory manuals and training courses. The organization wanted to develop a more system-atic approach to interviewing its UK customers, and developed an approach to verify the research that was done, to give senior management more confidence in the data that was being collected. The company's market was any company that needed health and safety, legal and regulatory information. Desk research revealed the following market universe:

Major corporations:	3,000 corporations
Middle market companies:	200,000 companies
Small companies (1–10 employees):	250,000 companies
Total universe:	453,000 companies

The company's internal sales data showed that the number of invoiced customers was 150,000, but this represented 66,000 invoiced companies, so its customer base was 15 per cent of the total market. Before undertaking this analysis the company had been selecting customers for interview without considering the type of company they worked for. So once this analysis had been completed it was decided to set up quotas in future surveys by classifying respondents as coming from major corporations, middle market companies or small companies.

However, it was realized that this classification was also limited. The research was intended to provide a basis for testing out new products, but the company did not know what proportion of the market were users of the different key products in the market. So it was decided to develop an 'establishment survey', a survey to establish the proportion of companies purchasing information products. 'Establishment survey' is the term for a survey conducted for the purpose of estimating the scale and characteristics of a potential market. Such a survey is important when setting up a panel, to help to determine the composition of the panel and to enable the calculation of weighting factors for use in grossing up (which is important when developing representation of market segments).

This survey assisted the publisher to define:

- the number of companies in different industries within the market;
- the number of different types of disciplines in the market;
- the characteristics of its existing customers, compared with other potential customers;
- the frequency of purchasing from them and other information providers;
- customers' perceptions and image of each company in the market;
- whether customers and potential customers were prepared to take part in future research.

Understanding this type of survey also enabled the publisher to develop a database of those prepared to take part in future research, thus enabling representative samples to be developed and used to monitor new product development and satisfaction with its products and services.

When developing trend data, previous studies covering similar research objectives guide a manager to select a sample size. The survey gives data on:

- the population of interest for the research;
- the likely response rate;
- the incidence rate of the product or service being researched;
- the number of market segments that are to be analysed.

GETTING THE MARKETING LANGUAGE CORRECT

As research has a primary objective of reducing risk by enabling organizations to understand what a market wants and how potential customers are likely to react to a product or service offered, it is important to relate all of the findings to the sales, marketing and communication strategy. A good manager will want these strategies to relate to the target customer and be oriented to the different customer types that exist in the target group. There are two research techniques that provide the right data and feedback to orient marketing effectively.

The first is to add into a questionnaire 'open-ended' questions that allow respondents – customers or potential customers – to express their likes, dislikes or attitude to the subject. Their answers give an indication of attitudes, motivations, reasons and 'true reaction' to the market, product or service. The best technique to use in research to identify how to increase sales through a customer-oriented strategy is to use this questioning process in two stages.

Initially, qualitative research is carried out by interviewing a small sample of respondents, who are asked open-ended questions such as 'Why?', 'What?', 'How?', 'When?' and Which?' This allows for a very detailed exploration of current buying habits, reasons for purchase and usage, and non-purchase and non-usage, and gives the manager the means of identifying how this background relates to the strategy being proposed. The results of this initial stage are therefore analysed with regard to how it helps a manager to focus the strategy more specifically. In the process there will be an urgent need to establish how significant these findings are for determining the priorities for implementing the strategy.

The second stage is to quantify the findings by asking many more respondents about the issues researched and identified in the first stage. A quantitative study is seen by some as just an attempt to confirm the findings of the qualitative phase by gaining agreement positively or negatively to the questions asked. However, this answer is not likely to be a detailed analysis or interpretation, and by limiting the answer to just 'Yes' or 'No' the manager could miss some of the context of the interpretation of the results.

The second technique is to create 'attitude' or 'image' or classification statements, which are used to establish the extent to which the respondent agrees with them. 'Attitude statements' are phrases or sentences that relate to the attitudes, motivations, and purchase and usage criteria that have been identified in the qualitative research. They are specifically phrased in the consumer's or customer's 'language' to help the strategy planner to orient the decisions in consumer terms. If we look at the map, atlas and travel guide market discussed earlier, the attitude statements might include:

> Maps are a hassle to us.
> I do not want to travel with a map as I do not want to look like a dumb tourist.
> I need landmark information to know where I am on the map.

Image statements are similar, but they relate to the image of the company, awareness of the company's activities via its marketing, or reaction to advertising, point-of-sale promotions, catalogues, direct mail or any other sales and marketing materials used by the company: for example 'forward looking product development', 'creative advertising', or 'good customer service'. Sample image statements for the health and safety information publisher discussed earlier are:

> Provides the most up to date information.
> Has a helpful telephone support line.

The researcher asks respondents whether they agree or disagree with the statement, or invites them to categorize it on an 'important' to 'unimportant' scale. If a five-point bipolar scale – two positive ratings, Agree and Agree Strongly, two negative ratings, Disagree and Disagree Strongly, and a don't know rating, Neither Agree nor Disagree – is used, the research analysis should provide useful data.

Two analyses can be achieved from this technique. A percentage response analysis is based on the total number of interviews and how many respondents agree or disagree with the statement. The other analysis is a mean (average) analysis based on the bipolar (+2 to –2) scale, which gives an average response to the rating. When you have a 'battery' of statements – a group of statements about which the respondent is asked in succession – the average analysis can provide a ranking of statements, which can be useful in assessing attitudes or motivations. This measures the extent to which certain factors are rated as important or unimportant by consumers.

An effective way of ensuring that the analysis is in the right language is to pose the question as though the consumer was in a conversation. In introducing the question the interviewer can imply that, as others have made a comment, it is useful to get a reaction to it: 'Some people have made comments about why they have bought maps. Looking at the statements listed on the questionnaire, please tell me whether you agree or disagree with them.' This can make an informant feel as if he or she is involved in the subject.

Attitude and image statements are the key to making research relate to marketing and communications planning. If research is carried out regularly, they can be used to monitor attitude and image change, and become an essential part of the research monitoring process. In recent years they have also been used for customer monitoring programmes, and their use in these has allowed more managers to benefit from this technique and discover how customer monitoring can influence strategy development and decision making. They are essential for developing comparative competitive analyses.

Elsewhere in the book we have referred to the application of techniques and their influence on management, and how they are used for planning. Attitude statements are an essential part of the application of techniques. Once quantified in a two-stage study, they have laid the 'benchmark', and if the survey is carried out again the results can be compared to show how attitudes change or trends are established.

Factor analysis can also be applied to the evaluation of the data collected from attitude statement assessment.

Computer generation of the statistical analysis using the appropriate statistical package correlates the attitudes of the informants and identifies a structure to the opinions given. This type of analysis assists the manager to advance from using standard socio-economic analysis to learning about and classifying the market in the context of both positive and negative attitudes and motivations.

Cluster analysis is a further approach to multivariate analysis, examining the relationships among a number of variables. This statistical technique aims to identify groups of individuals who have relatively similar characteristics, and distinguish these from any other individuals. So after having established the number of factors or attitudes and motivations through the factor analysis, the cluster analysis helps to define a specific target market or develop an effective market segmentation.

The key benefit of segmentation is to divide a market into parts, each of which has identifiable characteristics, whether they are of the product or service, or the user or buyer of the product. In the past 10 years this technique has again had a significant contribution to product planning and defining consumer characteristics to different markets, such as the ageing 'grey market', the gay and lesbian sector, and the African-American and Hispanic markets in the United States.

COLLECTING DATA IN THE COMPANY

Sometimes it is important to review the opinions of internal staff and research attitudes in the company. These surveys usually relate to remuneration packages or 'change management' to assess employees' attitudes to change. The following is a case example of an industrial company based in Chicago that did this to assess the effectiveness of the employee benefits package for its sales force. The sequence of activities was as follows:

1. It commissioned an independent professional research agency to conduct the survey.
2. A representative sample of 40 salespeople in each of the eight divisions was selected for interview. Each interview was an in-depth attitude evaluation lasting one hour, covering all aspects of the role of each employee and the remuneration package. The salespeople were given an incentive to participate, which included a summary of the results of the research.

3. The interviews were analysed and the major issues highlighted.
4. Through a quantification study, a self-completion postal question-naire was prepared for mailing to each of the 150 salespeople in the company. Provision was made for evaluating overall opinions on the major issues by listing a series of pre-coded questions. The questionnaires were colour coded by division, but otherwise they were anonymous and could not be traced to the respondent.
5. The returned questionnaires were analysed on the computer, and an analysis prepared detailing:
   - the common strengths of the sales job as perceived by the sales-people themselves;
   - specific strengths and weaknesses of the sales jobs in the various divisions;
   - the major issues concerning motivation, and what actions the salespeople expected from sales management to improve it;
   - the major issues concerning the sales force's morale and what actions the salespeople expected from sales management to improve it;
   - an assessment of the benefits package and what concerns they had.

The sales force questionnaire included the following:

- What opinion do you have of the company's:
   - advertising and sales promotion?
   - products and new products being planned?
   - sales supplies and materials (order forms, etc)?
- What is your opinion of the company's:
   - territorial arrangements for sales areas?
   - sales quotas by areas and products?
   - benefit package for salespeople?
   - bonus schemes and incentives?
- What is your opinion of your sales manager in terms of:
   - the support he provides?
   - his/her knowledge of your problems?
   - his/her overall contact with you?
   - the motivation he/she provides you?
- What is your opinion of top management in terms of:
   - awareness of the problems the sales force deal with?

- overall contact with you?
- support they provide?

Each question was rated using a five-point bipolar scale. The results of this employee opinion poll in the company were that:

- The total remuneration package was revised, because sales management had not appreciated the dissatisfaction caused by the various anomalies within the divisions.
- A new incentive scheme was devised to increase morale and motivation.
- Regular feedback was provided through news sheets, to give the sales force a broader awareness of what was happening in the company.

In this chapter we have seen how companies poll employees on attitudes to pay and conditions that could affect the level of service they provide. This has been taken a stage further by other companies as they have understood and compared the perceptions of staff towards their markets, the company and competitors, with those of the customers themselves.

CASE STUDIES: ASSESSING PURCHASING CRITERIA

This example is of three suppliers of industrial products who all needed to improve the margins achieved by their sales forces. Initially the senior management of all the companies believed the solution to their problem lay in negotiating an acceptable price. Research proved to the companies that price was not such a critical factor.

In the first company, a manufacturer of heavy machinery, management was convinced that its marketing strategy depended on effective pricing. As a result, sales training and field sales management resources were implemented with the sole aim of changing these attitudes. No one in the company tried to establish why it or its customers held such strong views on price.

The second company, suppliers of agricultural machinery, had had the same problem as the first company. However, its method of changing management's attitudes was to commission a study of customer buying attitudes. This was used to show the sales force why its views on pricing were wrong.

The third company, an industrial components supplier, approached the same problem by recognizing that if the opinions of customers and potential customers are fundamental to the sales effort, then so too are the views of the sales force. It compared the salespeople's perceptions of their customers and potential customers with data collected from research among customers. Both groups, of course, have definite reasons for holding their opinions. The way to progress was not to 'persuade' the sales force to change their opinions, but to rethink the approach of the company to the market. This involved the following:

- Changing sales attitudes by learning more about the customers.
- Restructuring patterns of customer contact.
- Developing a total company approach to 'putting the customer first'.
- Revising the whole method of communicating through direct contact, written communication and all forms of media promoting the company.

One engineering and automotive components company identified and listed the perceptions of customer purchasing criteria from both customers and salespeople in order of importance. The rankings were as follows (with the highest-ranked item first):

Customer ranking

Quality
Reliable delivery
Rapid delivery
Rapid enquiry handling
Price

Sales force ranking

Price
Quality

> Technical advice/support
> Reliable delivery
> Product range

This clearly shows that the salespeople were too price-conscious, and over-rated the customers' requirements for technical support and a comprehensive product range.

Discussions with the sales force and customers pointed to reasons for the conflicting points of view. The customers accepted that, while a good product range and technical service were available from all major suppliers, significant differences existed on reaction times to product availability and on reliability. Prices were accepted as comparable, and negotiation on price was used only as a purchasing technique with suppliers.

The salespeople were strongly influenced by the company's policy emphasizing product excellence and high levels of technical support capability. They had no direct contact with their order offices/delivery points, apart from problem chasing or checking up on orders from their sales areas. Much of their contact with customers was concerned with price negotiations. If either delivery or availability were mentioned, the query would be passed over to the relevant department.

So how could these differing perceptions be reconciled? The sales force needed a better understanding of the company's approach to order processing and delivery, as well as to become far more aware of the complexity of the buying process among its customers. This in turn would encourage 'non-sales' staff to become more involved in improving service levels, and also bring sales staff into contact with customers earlier in the sales process, in time to emphasize the high levels of product availability and good delivery service.

Implementation involved questioning what the company's product offering was, followed by strategy development and the creation of a more 'open' organization, including setting up better structures for effective communication and programmes to improve staff knowledge levels and involvement. The returns from a more confident sales force and service staff playing to their own strengths were considerable.

The implications of this type of approach are that management should not start with the premise that salespeople are automatically wrong in problem situations. For example, price is critical, although there are other, more important factors. The task is to explain why price is considered so important and what influences have contributed to it being so. The approach discussed earlier identifies how companies can differentiate between the techniques used by the sales force and the other marketing techniques adopted for their marketing strategies. It facilitates the most cost effective use of resources invested in the marketing mix, and puts emphasis behind those factors that have priority in customers' buying decisions.

ASSESSING CONSUMER BUYING BEHAVIOUR

Consumer buying behaviour is influenced by the following factors.

The culture in which the consumer lives

Consumers have values, perceptions, preferences and a behaviour pattern which are the result of environmental influences. Leisure habits, health factors and life style have as important an influence on buying behaviour as race, religion and nationality. Research helps to track cultural shifts that might suggest new ways to market and sell to consumers. Analysis of different cultural life styles also helps to identify both product and brand preferences. International research in the past used to concentrate on identifying the differences between consumers in different markets. Now, as more international marketing companies are developed, research is being used to understand the similarities between consumers in the global marketplace.

The social classification of the consumer

Consumer subcultures are classified by their patterns of occupation, income, education, wealth, and other variables that can be used to distinguish between different types of people. Research helps to develop marketing and sales campaigns that are targeted at the special attitudes, needs and perceptions of the different subgroups. This kind of classification also proves to be useful in identifying the differences in the buying behaviour between males and females in a family. For example, research shows that husbands tend to be dominant in taking decisions on life insurance, the choice of car and what television programmes to watch. Wives tend to be dominant in the choice of washing machine, carpeting and kitchenware. Husbands and wives make joint decisions when choosing living room furniture, where to go on holiday and where to live.

The personal characteristics of the consumer

Consumers' age, life-cycle stage, occupation, economic circumstances and personality influence the way in which they take buying decisions. Research assists in identifying consumer life styles, and provides management with the key to satisfying their needs.

The VALS™ (values and lifestyles) classification, developed in the United States, is an example of how people can be categorized through research, according to their life styles and personal characteristics. VALS is a marketing system that identifies current and future opportunities by segmenting the consumer marketplace on the basis of the personality characteristics that drive consumer behaviour. It uses psychology to analyse the dynamics underlying consumer preferences and choices. VALS not only distinguishes differences in motivation, it also captures the psychological and material constraints on consumer behaviour and,

- ideals, guided by knowledge and principles;
- achievement, looking for products and services that demonstrate success to their peers;
- self-expression: those who desire social or physical activity, variety, and risk.

A person's tendency to consume goods and services is influenced by factors that extend beyond age, income and education. Energy, self-confidence, intellectualism, novelty seeking, innovativeness, impulsiveness, leadership, and vanity play a critical role. VALS places US adult consumers into one of eight segments based on their responses to the VALS questionnaire.

Innovators

Innovators are successful, sophisticated, take-charge people with high self-esteem. Innovators are very active consumers, and their purchases reflect cultivated tastes for upscale, niche products and services.

Thinkers

Thinkers are motivated by ideals. They are mature, satisfied, comfortable and reflective people who value order, knowledge and responsibility. Thinkers are conservative, practical consumers; they look for durability, functionality and value in the products they buy.

Achievers

Motivated by the desire for achievement, Achievers have goal-oriented lifestyles and a deep commitment to career and family. Achievers live conventional lives, are politically conservative, and respect authority and the status quo. Achievers are active in the consumer marketplace – they favour established, prestige products and services that demonstrate success to their peers.

Experiencers

Experiencers are motivated by self-expression. They are avid consumers and spend a comparatively high proportion of their income on fashion, entertainment and socializing. Their purchases reflect the emphasis they place on looking good and having 'cool' stuff.

Believers

Believers are motivated by ideals. They are conservative, conventional people with concrete beliefs based on traditional, established codes: family, religion, community and the nation. As consumers, Believers are predictable; they choose familiar products and established brands.

Strivers

Strivers are trendy and fun loving. Strivers are active consumers because shopping is both a social activity and an opportunity to demonstrate to peers their ability to buy. As consumers, they are as impulsive as their financial circumstance will allow.

Makers

Makers are motivated by self-expression. They are unimpressed by material possessions other than those with a practical or functional purpose. As they prefer value to luxury, they buy basic products.

Survivors

Survivors live narrowly focused lives. They are cautious consumers. They represent a very modest market for most products and services. They are loyal to favourite brands, especially if they can purchase them at a discount.

VALS™ is provided by an employee-owned spin-off of the former Stanford Research Institute, www.sric-bi.com

The psychological influences on the consumer

It is important for management to analyse what motivates consumers by assessing their image and perceptions of a company, identifying how they become aware of products and how their attitudes are changed by advertising and communications.

RESEARCHING BEHAVIOURAL CHARACTERISTICS OF CONSUMERS

Getting to know the needs of consumers almost guarantees success in marketing. Determining how buyers go through the decision making process provides marketing management with all they need to know about selling a product the consumer wants to buy. It can be useful to build a predictive model of the behaviour of an individual. The information required to build and illustrate the model includes:

- the behaviour, beliefs and attitudes of consumers;
- the extent to which they are aware of choices;
- the importance they attach to different product brand characteristics;
- any constraints that might exist on buying behaviour.

In assessing consumer buying behaviour, then, the most important research activities are:

- To collect and analyse data relating to the habits, attitudes and needs of consumers, with a view to sorting consumers into homogeneous groups differentiated by their life styles and buying behaviour.
- To collect and analyse data relating to the products, services or brands that are available in the market. This helps to focus on how these are perceived by consumers, with a view to sorting the brands into groups of those with 'like attributes' as perceived by the consumer.
- To collect and analyse data relating to the awareness of the products and services. This helps to focus on which consumers are the current market, and which are the potential markets that need to be influenced and persuaded to buy the product.

BUYERS' CHARACTERISTICS AND BUYING DECISIONS

It is important to identify the characteristics of buyers and their buying decision processes, in order to target them with the most appropriate marketing methods. Management needs to gain an understanding of how their characteristics and decision making processes relate to the products or services they choose; the brand they select; the outlet at which they buy the product; the time it takes them to decide which products to buy; and the amount purchased.

To assess how buying decisions are made, it is necessary to identify the criteria used for buying products and the level and type of influence on the buyer.

Buying roles

Several different roles have been defined in the consumer buying process:

- the Initiator: the first person to think of the idea of buying a particular product;
- the Influencer: the person who influences others in taking the final decision to purchase;
- the Decider: the person who takes the key decision;

■ the Buyer: the person who makes the actual purchase;
■ the User: the consumer or the user;

Buying behaviour

Buying behaviour divides into different types: routine buying, initial problem solving, and extended problem solving. The marketing response will be different in each case.

Routine buying

The consumer purchases low-cost goods frequently, and does not give much thought to the purchase. Marketing management will want to ensure continuing customer satisfaction by maintaining the product's quality, service and value. New customers will also be attracted through promotions, which emphasize the product's acceptability and point out its specific features and benefits.

Initial problem solving

The consumer might be interested in another product brand/product class, but does not know too much about it. He or she will ask specific questions at the point of sale about the product, or will look to advertising and promotions to learn more about its specific features and benefits. An advertising campaign should be created aimed at increasing consumers' awareness and developing product familiarity.

Extended problem solving

The consumer might be interested in buying a specific product in a product line about which he or she has little or no knowledge. It is important to ascertain what criteria are used in solving the problem of which product to buy. Marketing management needs to understand these criteria to ensure that all communications convey the attributes of the products appreciated by the consumers.

Examining the purchasing process

The purchasing process can be broken down into five different stages: problem recognition, information search, evaluation of alternatives, the purchasing decision, and post-purchase behaviour. Research should be carried out at each of these stages, to arm the marketing manager with information and guidance on the most appropriate marketing response for each stage.

Problem recognition

The initial stage is recognition by the consumer of a need to be filled, or problem to be solved, by the purchase of a product. Research identifies what needs or problems consumers have, what caused them and how they led to the product being chosen. Gathering this data helps the marketing manager to identify what most often motivates interest in the product category. Then he or she will be able to develop marketing communications that stimulate the interest. This type of research is usually qualitative research.

Research is used by companies marketing the products to identify which sources of information are evaluated and how they are rated. Typical research will assess:

- how consumers first heard about the product and the brands of products;
- what information they received;
- how they decided to rank the importance of the various information sources;
- what criteria were ranked;
- what their overall reactions were to the information and how it persuaded them to buy the product.

This type of research is generally initially qualitative and then quantitative research. After this assessment, a company can develop the appropriate communications campaign aimed at its potential markets.

Evaluation of the alternatives

Consumers decide between one product and another by comparing the various characteristics and attributes of the different products. Research techniques are used to encourage consumers to assess:

- the product's attributes;
- 'importance weightings' for these attributes;
- the consumers' beliefs about the product;

- the product's utility functions;
- the ways in which consumers evaluate the products and their attributes.

Consumers will obviously pay most attention to the attributes that most closely reflect their needs. Research helps to identify those market segments that are most likely to be attracted to the particular attributes of a product. It is therefore important to research the motivations of buyers, to find out how they actually evaluate product and brand alternatives. This research is also initiated through qualitative research, then the main factors are quantified.

Different marketing responses to consumer product evaluation could be to:

- redesign the product to ensure it has all the characteristics potential buyers expect and, indeed, need to ensure they buy the product;
- change the perception of the product or service, by emphasizing some of its features or benefits;
- change the consumer's beliefs about competitors' brands by emphasizing the benefits of one product over another;
- change the weights given to the different product attributes, to show that, for example, the size of the product might bring added benefits to a consumer;
- emphasize attributes that potential purchasers do not readily identify.

Purchasing decision

Management should also be aware of less predictable influences over the purchasing decision, such as the attitude of others to the product. For example, although a man might choose one product his spouse might suggest that a cheaper or more expensive product would be better. The need to economize, and the opportunity to spend a little more, can be significant.

Post-purchase behaviour

After the product has been bought management needs to know about customers' reactions and whether or not their expectations were met. Market research at this stage will, of course, establish how effective the marketing and sales operation has been.

CONSUMER BEHAVIOUR CLASSIFICATIONS

Most market and media research studies collect a mass of data about consumers and their characteristics. Typically, this survey data has been analysed on single dimensions such as age, sex, income, and social class. The purpose of recording such information is to evaluate a consumer in terms of his or her type of purchasing behaviour. The social grade classifications of A, B, C1, C2, D, E are based on the occupational status of the head of the household. The value of this classification has been eroded by the increasing number of families with two or more income earners, and by the redistribution of income and purchasing power across the defined classes. This limits the definition of target markets, and any further detail has to come from cross-tabulation or segmentation computations that adds to the cost of the research. It is here that lifestyle classifications are beneficial.

SAGACITY

To circumvent this problem, SAGACITY (a special analysis of the national readership survey) has been developed in the UK. SAGACITY is a single-dimension classification readily tabulated to provide additional classifications, which give newer insights into consumer behaviour. It helps to define the target markets by measuring consumers' actual behaviour in each product field of interest in total, and within SAGACITY groups. Demographic criteria have been combined, enabling respondents to be placed into one of 12 groups. These groups are designed to be as homogeneous as possible, containing consumers at similar stages in their life cycle and with similar disposable income and cultural characteristics. These different SAGACITY groups are found to exhibit differing behaviour patterns over a wide range of markets. They reveal the actual nature of those markets, permitting the development of good target market definitions. The 12 groups also exhibit widely differing media usage habits, and therefore offer a high level of discrimination between media.

The basic thesis of the SAGACITY groupings is that people acquire different aspirations and behaviour patterns as they go through their life cycle. The four main stages of the life cycle of adults aged over 15 are defined as follows (this example is taken from a specific survey year to show the relevant penetration figures):

- The dependent stage: 16 per cent of all adults; describes consumers who are still living in their parents' household or studying full time if they live away from home.
- The pre-family stage: 8 per cent of all adults; consists of adults under 35 years old who have already established their own households, but as yet have no children.
- The family stage: 36 per cent of all adults consist of families with one or more children, and a head of household under 65.
- The late stage: includes all adults whose children have already left home, or who are 35 or older and childless.

The other elements of the SAGACITY groupings are related to the income and occupational characteristics of the individual or couple forming the household. The income breakdown is applied only at the family stage and the late stage. This division by income rather than economic activity is particularly important at the late stage, as there is a significant minority of retired people who are classified into the 'better off' income grouping and who might be expected to exhibit similar consumption patterns to those who are still working. The last element used to form the 12 SAGACITY groups is the occupation of the head of the household. Individuals are grouped into non-manual (white collar) occupations (ABCls) and manual (blue collar) occupations (C2DEs).

ACORN

ACORN (A Classification Of Residential Neighbourhoods) is another international system for targeting customers by their life styles. Developed initially in the UK, this system divides blocks of 150 addresses throughout the country into 54 different types of neighbourhood, according to their demographic, housing and socio-economic characteristics. The system is based on an analysis of published statistics from the 1981, 1991 and 2001 censuses, and is being updated from the 1991 census.

The usefulness of this system is that it enables manufacturers and service providers to use their own customer address records, rather than rely on surveys to identify the types of area where they make the highest sales. They can also target their advertising expenditure, using only the media that are more effective in reaching their key ACORN type customers. Companies that have used customer addresses to define ACORN types range from direct mail companies, financial organizations which hold addresses for every account holder, gas and electricity and television companies which keep accounting information, retailers who operate credit card facilities, travel companies, motor appliance and furniture manufacturers who retain names and addresses for warranty or guarantee purposes, to charities and also political parties.

ACORN is used by insurance companies, building societies, credit operators and direct mail houses to identify the types of customer it is most profitable to service. They can identify from their own records which are the most loyal customers, in which parts of the country average order values are the highest, where bad debts are the lowest and where responsiveness to mailshots is the most effective.

ACORN analyses also show that building societies are better placed than banks to deliver financial services to areas of population growth. There are some 5,000 building society branches and 12,000 banks nationwide, but the penetration of these varies widely across the country. In areas of high population growth the banks face stiff competition from building societies.

Use of the ACORN system

The classifications have proved to be very useful in determining the characteristics of different customer groups. For example, 'High Status' Retirement areas are usually poor on expenditure per capita, but good on loyalty. Modern Council Estates are good on mailing responsiveness, but bad on debt. It is also possible to determine the different types of areas by assessing the age distribution. The analysis identifies:

- pre-family areas, of relatively high disposable income and low commitments;
- young family areas, with a high level of mortgage, hire purchase and overdraft use;
- post family areas, with a high level of savings, low use of credit and high incomes;
- retirement areas, with low income, but significant investment income.

ACORN has become widely used in market research, advertising and direct marketing to improve marketing targeting. It is also of use to sales managers for setting equitable sales targets for different sales territories. Until now the sales manager has had to take subjective decisions about the sales potential of various territories, and has not had a definitive mechanism for setting sales quotas. Now, however, using ACORN and analysing customer addresses, the sales manager can set a sales target by each ACORN type. This extends to allowing for the population in each ACORN type within the sales territories. Quotas can now be set to relate to the potential for business in each area.

One other important application is 'site location', using information about ACORN profiles of each shopping centre to minimize the risk of opening an unprofitable shop. Retailers such as W H Smith and Boots are known to use ACORN to evaluate the product ranges that should be stocked at different stores in different parts of the country.

CONCLUSION

Once the basic physical characteristics of the market have been identified, it is essential, in order to understand consumer behaviour, to discover the reasons for people's actions, what motivates and influences them:

- Why do people act in certain ways?
- Why do they hold certain opinions?
- Why have they developed certain attitudes?
- How have their lifestyles influenced their behaviour?
- Why do they have certain preferences?

Marketing is concerned with change, adapting to change and creating change. Current and historic spending and savings patterns may provide a basis for market prediction. A healthy sales and profit record for a product, which has represented the best rationalized compromise available of customer needs and customer satisfaction, may be to little avail if a new product, nearer the customer's perception of the ideal, becomes available. Thus continuous analysis of consumer buying behaviour and decision making helps management to understand the consumer better, to market products the consumer wants, and to ensure that the total marketing effort is consumer-oriented. Identifying and measuring consumer attitudes is effectively one of the most important benefits of using market research techniques to improve marketing.

Research, then, can help to improve the sales and selling process, as its practical application makes a positive contribution to management thinking and policy making.

The principles and techniques of research can be used to a greater extent in the future to evaluate, assess and improve the sales and marketing methods of any company. Specifically, research can be applied to help to improve the sales process by:

- aiding the overall marketing and sales planning activities, which highlight how the sales activity should be carried out;
- determining whether the communications process is supported, extended and enhanced by the abilities; establishing whether the sales process is being completed with the maximum efficiency and optimum effectiveness by the sales force.

CASE STUDY: USING RESULTS TO INFLU-ENCE THE MARKET SUCCESSFULLY

There are two examples. The first company is involved in supplying artificial flavourings to major food producers. Its main competitor was a company marketing 'natural flavourings'. In reality, both products were derived from natural raw materials, with the lead company only reprocessing the product to allow ease of use and greater consistency for its customers' processes. As a result it was the market leader. However, the competitor tried to emphasize its products' 'natural state', despite the fact that productivity gains obtained from the processed product were advantageous to the user, and no apparent difference could be detected in the final end product, so far as the producer was concerned.

The lead company's American counterpart was experiencing major marketing problems with a similar situation in its home market. Again, there was an alternative 'natural product' produced by a company that successfully used this 'natural' profile. As a result of exchange rate changes, it was possible that this American product would become available at a competitive price in the UK, marketed according to this natural profile.

The UK company, recognizing the impending competition from the US product and the possible resurgence of its domestic competition, questioned how this would affect its market. It therefore briefed a market research consultancy to analyse the situation and recommend what activities should be undertaken to protect its markets. It became clear that there was no data on what the real effect of the flavouring was on the product, beyond the normal technical use. The research consultancy suggested a programme of market research to examine any differences in the three flavourings within the product, in the opinions of the user and the consumer but not the manufacturer.

Conventional consumer quantitative research through hall testing was carried out with all three product variants. The expected outcome of the research was that the consumer would perceive no difference and that 'naturalness' would not be an issue. In fact the research, although confirming this latter issue, did not give an even result between the variants, but suggested that the end product with the lead company's flavouring gave an 'added quality' to the product.

The lead company was now in a very strong position to action these results in an aggressive marketing campaign, designed to show its retail customers that their consumers could differentiate between flavourings and that its product was preferred. The outcome of the research gave a leading edge to the UK company, and this was subsequently marketed very efficiently to its benefit.

It is also worth commenting that had the market research findings been negative to the UK company, it would nevertheless have been ready to establish a technical research and development programme to overcome any product deficiencies, so the company had planned to use the research effectively. Clearly, the market research was the linchpin of the company's decision making process, and the results led to successful marketing activity.

In this situation, the company had recognized a marketing problem, had explored the extent of the problem through market research, and when the results were obtained, used them to influence its market significantly.

HINTS ON USING THE BEST RESEARCH TECHNIQUES

- Decide on how to reduce uncertainty in decision making by recognizing that published research and external surveys can provide both interesting and actionable information.
- Take as much time as possible and as long as is practicable for the discussion and development of the research. The longer that planning is carried out, the better the result of the project.
- Published information should be collected to add to the intelligence in the company, but do not depend on it as the key to decision making. It is likely not to be totally relevant or sufficiently accurate to be related to the sales, marketing or communications plan.
- Link the data generated on your computer with published data, as this will provide sufficient information to develop trend data, based on company performance analysis (actual sales and so on). Add to it the key findings of your regular survey research and it will provide the benchmark for an interactive marketing intelligence system.
- Use brand share data to indicate the effectiveness of sales and marketing methods. The brand share analysis should be viewed as the 'early warning system' for further market analysis, depending on the brand movements identified.
- When profiling the market through survey research, ensure there are sufficient questions in the questionnaire to sub-segment the target groups into useful analyses. Do not do what a retailer did recently in trying to segment its market. It chose to divide it into heavy, medium and light buyers based on the number of products they bought (heavy – 10-plus products; medium – 5 to 10 products; light – 1 to 4 products). This is less effective than making these definitions based on use and purchase, as it does not give any information on buying habits and the frequency of buying. A better classification of purchase might be, heavy – a few times a year or more frequent; medium – once a year to one and a half years; light – once every two years or less frequent. Usage might be classified as heavy – once a week or more; medium – a few times a month; light – a few times every six months/a few times a year or less.
- Customizing data means analysing the research in relation to the sales decisions, marketing plans and communications strategies that are being developed.

■ When completing research on competitive positioning, ask what opinion consumers have of [the following companies] in terms of their:
   - products and product range, and new product development ability;
   - pricing, discounts and special price promotions;
   - packaging and new packaging development ability;
   - point of sales materials;
   - salespeople and their willingness to be of assistance;
   - sales office staff and their efficiency in dealing with orders and queries;
   - telephone sales personnel and their efficiency.

■ Ask consumers to think about the suppliers from whom they usually purchase your products. Do they consider them to have:
   - a modern or old-fashioned image?
   - ability to lead the market?
   - a good product range or limited product range?
   - forward product development?
   - acceptable margins?
   - good salespeople?
   - sufficient sales calls?
   - good delivery lead times?

■ Ask how customers and potential customers behave.
■ Ask whether their buying decisions might change, and what would influence this change.
■ Ask how they make the decisions about the products they buy and the services they use.
■ Ask whether these decisions are the same for competitors' products.
■ Ask how consumers are motivated towards buying products.
■ Ask how consumers first become aware of the product.
■ Ask what the consumer considers to be the main differences between the company's products and other products on the market.
■ Ask which product attributes are the main ones in influencing the consumer to buy products.
■ Check whether customers are classified according to their life styles.

4 What to measure and how to measure it

INTRODUCTION

The task of data collection is not complete until a manager has turned the information that is collected in the research into actionable facts, that lead to conclusions and then practical recommendations that help to take decisions to enable a company to increase sales. There is a sequence to this data analysis process.

First, the data has to be edited and coded. Editing removes omissions and errors, and also provides the opportunity to find inconsistencies. Coding is the method for deciding on how the data is assembled into common factors, which can be analysed and entered into a computer, and used to interpret sales and marketing actions.

Managers should not really decide what to measure until the basic analysis techniques are applied, to see whether the classification information provides a meaningful analysis. This provides the data user with the first results of the research, and establishes whether the market can be segmented, or certain subgroups show any strength of opinion in the market. Typically, this can be achieved by providing one computer tabular analysis for each question being analysed from a questionnaire.

It is only once these tabulations have been reviewed that a manager can decide to apply statistical techniques that will help to understand the facts that have been collected in a more meaningful way. If a survey is carried out regularly, then the applied techniques can be run at the initial analysis of the new survey and updated for each of the following surveys.

The most efficient manager will want to evaluate some options for what to measure and how to measure the data. These include the following:

Identifying segments from the results

Data analysis can identify the size and nature of subgroups of the population. It can confirm how the subgroups buy and use products, and their attitudes to the companies manufacturing and selling them. As markets become more 'global', the segmentation analyses will be used more frequently, as they are important in establishing what similarities and differences exist in markets in the global village. The advantage of global marketing is to be able to find similarities in the different markets the company is operating in.

Using data for forecasting

Existing data can be analysed with past data, trends can be identified and highlighted, and then a forecast developed by projecting the trend forward. When initial forecasts have been proved useful, more detailed forecasts can be developed by developing 'market models', which make assumptions that there are relationships with the data being forecast and factors that have influence on the data such as economic, political or financial factors.

Applying forecasting models to the data

Data that does not show any trend or seasonality is most effectively analysed by applying forecasting models such as moving averages. Seasonal patterns are best evaluated through special techniques for exponential smoothing.

Using attitude and behaviour models

These include 'trade-off' models, pricing models and test market models.

Conjoint analysis is effective for analysing experimental data. It models the decision process that consumers take when selecting a product or service, and relates their own data to the decision process.

Price modelling provides all the facts about buyers and relates consumers' reactions to pricing, establishing the most acceptable price to the buyers. Test market models forecast the potential for a new product, by estimating brand share depending on variations of the marketing mix.

Using data fusion

This is 'fusing' together data from two surveys or even between two segments of a market. The first survey is described as the 'donor survey', which is transferred to the second survey, the 'recipient survey'. The fusion process depends on statistical calculations, which measure the similarities between the two surveys. When all similarities have been analysed, the rest of the data stands alone for further analysis to establish its significance. Data fusion is only effective if the surveys can be matched or have been carried out using similar sampling and analysis techniques.

Analysing data

Good analysis of data depends on good questionnaire design, as unless the data collection method is well laid out, it is likely to be difficult to analyse the data collected. The basic method for analysis is a cross-tabulation which cross-analyses each question in the questionnaire with the key variables in the market – socio-economic classification, computer user, regular user of the Internet, area of the country or whatever factor is being researched. These are likely to provide 'top line' information, but there may not be sufficient detail for an in-depth understanding of the market or consumers' attitudes to the product. More complex techniques start with multivariate techniques used in survey research. They relate to three different uses:

Developing a segmentation analysis

Factor analysis is a technique that analyses the answers to a battery of questions, whether they are attitude or image statements. It groups the questions that have been answered, and links data that has similarities. Cluster analysis is a similar technique, which groups respondents who answer questions in the same manner. The data analysis therefore identifies the segments that exist within the data.

Using a preference analysis

Conjoint analysis is typically used to determine whether one factor is more important to a consumer than another. This might, for example, relate to package style compared with the size of a pack in which a product is packaged, analysing which type of pack a consumer prefers.

Applying complex forecasting techniques

These are mainly multiple regression techniques, which analyse the relationship between one dependent variable and a group of variables, which are 'predictors'. The simplest form of the technique is time series analyses.

All of the above techniques are available to the numerate manager and those interested in applying computer packages. The most effective way of measuring results is to develop the data analysis into a graphic presentation. Even the non-numerate manager cannot fail to appreciate the results of a survey if they are clearly laid out in graphic format. Most computer software packages include a graphics package, and all are easy to use for the non-technical computer user. A PowerPoint presentation is very effective for showing data and the key segments that are important.

APPLYING ANALYSIS TECHNIQUES TO DECISION MAKING

Most surveys reveal that one sub-group has a greater preference for a product or is more active in a market than the rest of the defined consumers. It is therefore both logical and important to segment the market, to gain a greater understanding of the opportunities for targeting by understanding the nature and characteristic of the target segment.

The segmentation measures that are most effective in measuring research survey results are the following.

Socio-economic classifications

These are sex, age and social class gradings to describe the characteristics of the consumer. The importance here is not just to analyse the information, but also to make up groupings that have a significant meaning in sales and marketing terms. One such grouping is a life-cycle analysis – early stage, family stage and late stage – relating the ages of consumers to their likes and dislikes, and showing how these change with age progression.

Geographic classifications

These are typical segmentation criteria that can be applied to any market. This field has become more interesting in the past few years as more detailed geodemographics systems have been developed. These will be covered later in this chapter.

Consumer behaviour analysis

The most effective way to analyse the market is to segment it according to current and potential customers, or those consumers who are aware and not aware of the product or manufacturer. This behavioural analysis provides much more meaningful analyses than a basic socio-economic classification.

Analysing data has, in essence, become more difficult for the user as there are now so many different techniques available. The user has to decide what is needed. Careful and well-thought-out use of the techniques will enable managers to make the data they need both relevant and actionable information.

Use and purchase classifications

One recent trend is the classification of data by the type of use of a product or service. This allows the data to relate more directly to different users in the market and their behaviour. Analysis of this type tends to assist in assessing and re-specifying consumer communication, highlighting product and service benefits and improving media targeting.

Computer techniques

There are some analysis techniques that are becoming very effective in the management of information and which managers are finding useful. Research and information is becoming more useful to them for planning and monitoring sales, marketing and communications as a result.

GEODEMOGRAPHICS

The most significant development of the application and use of existing data is geodemographics. The technique of geodemographics is to take the information from the census data in any country and re-analyse it for any interesting application that is available. For example, a few years ago the Irish Trade Board completed an analysis of the census to identify the location of the Irish-born residents in the United Kingdom, to plan direct marketing for Irish manufacturers and suppliers. Its most effective use is to provide research and marketing personnel with the means to both understand and target consumers effectively.

Geodemographics originated in the United States in the 1970s, when the US Navy had experienced recruitment problems. The Navy took the US census data to identify large population concentrations of young males eligible for recruitment. Identifying them by the state, town and areas they lived in, the US Navy developed promotional campaigns in the areas identified.

UK geodemographics date back to 1979 when a census-based geodemographics system was developed called ACORN (A Classification of Residential Neighbourhoods). The system has 54 neighbourhood types clustered into 17 specific groups. It is based on the assumption that people who live in similar areas – in terms of housing and surroundings – are likely to have similar behavioural, purchasing and lifestyle habits. Manufacturers and service companies can then target their products and services to the similar areas that have been identified.

The initial and successful application of the technique has been for the retail sector, which has used it to define branch catchment areas, new site and relocation analysis, and target customer promotions for discount schemes and special offers. What is interesting about geodemographics is the trend analysis that it is now providing, which measures the affluence of target customer types and how this changes over a period of time.

Other very effective users of geodemographic classification systems have been the financial services sectors. Banks, building societies, insurance companies, investment advisers and stockbrokers have all used some aspect of the data for cross-selling and to analyse the areas around branch networks. An application for ACORN is the pinpoint analysis in the UK of the financial services sector's financial research survey. The analysis is based on the findings of the financial survey, and it looks at the way people behave in terms of money – whether they have shares, bank accounts, investment trusts, pension funds and so on – and uses this analysis to develop neighbourhood discriminators and characteristics.

One of the problems that now exists with regard to geodemographics is that there is a number of competing systems available, making the decision which to use a complex one. The most significant development for the industry has been the advance in computer technology, allowing PC-based programs to do complete, detailed and complex analyses. The development of PC-based geographic information systems (GIS) has been the most significant development, allowing data to be mapped and analysed visually. The more advanced companies in applying computer techniques merge the geodemographic data with their own internal information and other external data, for customer and market modelling and profiling on their own marketing information systems. Typical use of these techniques is by local government and utilities.

The argument for geodemographic information relates to its accuracy and relevance to the user. The importance of lifestyle information from survey research is that it represents actual information on a specific product purchasing and consumption habit, relating the data to the consumer needs and changing trends in the market. But most of these surveys are representative sample surveys, and the lifestyle data coverage, in terms of both its geography and its socio-economic spread, is limited to representatives of the population.

A geodemographic system can provide total representation, as every household in the country returns a census form to the government. Various parts of the classification of this information are used for marketing purposes:

■ Owner occupancy provides important marketing factors, such as disposable income and negative equity.

- Multiple car ownership provides an indicator of the degree of affluence of the household.
- Ethnic origin is important for identifying niche markets and specialist sectors for specific products and services.
- Occupation of householders relates to their background, interests and buying habits.
- Mode of transport to work gives an indication of the household's mobility and needs in each part of the country.
- Socio-economic classification gives an important profile of consumer status and likely affluence.

When the above types of data are combined, then the ability to target products, markets and geographical or regional marketing campaigns is increased. ACORN itself has developed its services for specific targeting. Household ACORN provides direct marketers with the facility to understand and reach individual householders within a neighbourhood. Investor ACORN combines data on share ownership to target consumers who are more likely to spend on top of the range and luxury products. Arts ACORN combines data on people who attend arts events, to help arts venues to target likely customers more effectively.

Using geodemographics to grow your business

As the competitive environment increases in all markets, more and more marketing management will use geodemographics and lifestyle analyses. Geodemographics are effective if they are used in the marketing information system with other classification systems, such as the standard system for age, sex and social class. Geodemographics have strength in their use for understanding the characteristics of the market, using a postcode analysis, and giving precise and detailed targeting. Lifestyle analyses have become effective in direct marketing, as they provide mailing lists of target consumers of 'like' characteristics.

The geodemographic systems that exist are:

- ACORN – a classification of residential neighbourhoods based on 54 neighbourhood clusters.
- PiNPoint – pinpoints identified neighbourhoods, and also overlays Ordnance Survey data.

- FiNPiN – a market-specific classification developed on the basis of consumer research into consumers' financial activities from the Financial Research Survey.
- CCN's MOSAIC – over 55 neighbourhood types grouped into 10 lifestyle groups.

These lifestyle databases are available to management through list rental services. The impact of their availability in the market has been to draw a very careful distinction between these systems and market research data. Lifestyle data collects information on the products people buy, but also provides the actual names of respondents for marketing, which under the Code of Conduct of the Market Research Society contravenes the parts of the code that provide reassurance of confidentiality when carrying out survey research. Use of these services therefore has to be defined carefully, and where possible survey research and direct marketing should not overlap as a direct relationship of the analysis.

The main use of these classifications systems is for both identifying and profiling the customer base – where they are and who they are. Geodemographic profiles are profiles of the neighbourhood within which customers live. Profiling a customer database against a lifestyle analysis means the two databases have to be matched. Key applications giving an address with a postcode, and attaching a neighbourhood classification, are:

- sales customers databases;
- rented mailing lists of customer types;
- door-to-door targeting for direct mail;
- user and attitude research in certain neighbourhood types;
- retail catchment area analysis;
- sales territory analysis and allocation.

Geographical information systems (GIS) are computer-based systems for storing and using information that can be related to specific locations or areas. In the context of geodemographics and lifestyle analyses, GIS are the delivery systems for reports and maps, which the user might require.

Geodemographics will grow as more data becomes available and customized classifications are developed for market sector and product groups. These developments will relate to better door-to-door distribution and trade marketing for targeted localized marketing activity. GIS will stimulate this, as they become the central operating and focal point of the marketing information system.

MARKET MAPPING

It might sound rather obvious to a manager, but there are benefits to market mapping, in understanding the extent of the market the company is operating in and the performance of the company's products at all levels in the structure of the map. However, there are two definitions of market mapping and both have to be clearly identified, to clarify how the maps are constructed and how the information they provide is used. What is important for both applications of market mapping is that management sees them as another addition to the marketing information in understanding either the success of the products the company sells in the market, or how the customers can be classified into different target groups, which relate to how they appreciate or respond to the product benefits.

Managers use 'market maps' to establish clearly all levels of the distribution network, define what they sell, identify sales at all levels and if mapped on a regular basis establish specific trends in the different types of distributor; and to define target customers by relating their attitudes to product benefits – what they like and what they dislike – with the consumer classifications that are used in the market.

The most effective classifications are those that segment the customer base according to lifestyle or life preference classification – those that are descriptive of the habits, activities and interests of consumers. Although these have been developed by advertising agencies in some markets and used as general descriptions, most companies need to analyse their own survey data to make this type of market analysis effective. Typical lifestyle classifications in the 1980s have developed terminology such as 'Yuppies', 'Dinkies' and other such descriptions of the type of consumer they are trying to describe. (A yuppie is a young up and coming professional person.) Now they have been developed in many parts of the world, and it is interesting to see how they differ in different countries.

Market mapping is the first stage in setting up the market information system. It helps managers to:

- define clearly the size and shape of their markets and those components that constitute the market;
- determine how the various levels or components of the market in the map relate to each other;
- specify each of the sales, marketing and communications methods that are used for effective selling at each part of the distribution network, and monitoring the success of these methods.

In the competitive markets of the new century, market mapping has become even more important in understanding the structure and nature of the trends in each of the segments. It is also effective in helping to develop the more creative aspect of sales, marketing and communications planning, as it creates a better opportunity for communicating to the target market more in the context of people's lifestyles and habits.

The use of mapping is therefore effective for developing sales messages; strap lines for advertising and other communications, and also in identifying, establishing and developing brand strategies. Brand mapping is being used by consumer goods markets to stimulate purchase and develop consumer loyalty to the purchase and repurchase of brands. It is therefore an analysis technique, which helps a manager to understand the market and the behaviour of the customer in the market much more clearly, increasing the chance of taking consumer-oriented decisions.

CASE STUDY

A government tourist office: mapping the market to understand tourists' needs more clearly

The role of a government tourist office is to define the market for attracting visitors to the country it represents among the travelling public of the country it is operating in. It has to develop a marketing campaign that promotes the country, its features, its travel facilities and all aspects of what makes it attractive to a leisure or business visitor.

Our case study concentrates on a European country promoting its facilitiés, attractions and tourist areas in the UK. This European country is advanced in culture and leisure facilities, and was aware that it is not promoting itself effectively, as the number of visitors to the country from the UK was not showing sufficient growth. As a result, it approached market research organizations to establish which companies could assist it in collecting information on potential travellers, in making its advertising and promotional campaign more effective, and in persuading holidaymakers to travel to the country.

Two aspects of the market analysis were required. First, the number of travellers to the country had to be identified from government statistics, to identify whether there was a growth or decline in the number visiting the country. In this instance the number was static, and this indicated an opportunity for stimulation of an interested or loyal market.

The second aspect was to define the profile of the market, but to establish the segmentation in terms of those who knew the country well and visited it frequently, those who knew it and stayed there on the way to other countries, and those who were not visiting it but could be persuaded to take a holiday there.

The segmentation also had to take account of two other factors that were important for marketing the country as a destination. Leisure travel can be divided into travel for short breaks – a visit that is less than four nights – and vacation visits that are four nights or more. There is also the additional visit, which can be taken with one of the other options if a person visits a country more than once a year. The other more complex part of the segmentation analysis was relative to the marketing of the regions of the country. Could these be promoted competitively for their facilities and the types of vacation that they could offer – active or inactive – depending on consumers' interests and lifestyles? The choice included culture and the arts, leisure and the beach, eating and drinking fine foods and wine, or pursuing specific sports such as swimming, skiing, riding and water skiing.

The project was divided into three stages:

- A qualitative phase through group discussions, to understand how travellers select a leisure destination and why they would or would not visit the country being researched.
- A further qualitative evaluation of only those people who had travelled to the various regions of the country.
- Full market quantification through in-home interviews (400 travellers who had visited the country and 400 travellers who had not visited the country).

The staged project provided the government tourist office with a number of benefits for building up the data collection and analysis, by deciding what the data was saying in the context of market needs and how it would use the data. What was apparent from the stages of the research was how the tourist office understood the attitudes of the traveller and potential traveller to the country. The qualitative analysis showed that there were few differences between age or socio-economic classifications, as people would travel to the country for cheap short breaks, and also go there for their annual vacations. The analysis of the qualitative data implied that the attitude and image statements that were required, and had to be created from this analysis, needed to relate to the consumer needs for allocating their time when at their destination in the country.

These statements were added to the questionnaires for the two surveys of 400 informants each. Initial analysis of these confirmed the issues identified in the qualitative research, and also provided the ranking of their importance for including them in the promotion of the country. But as the lack of age and socio-economic segmentation was confirmed, it became essential to make a more detailed and market-oriented analysis.

Two analyses were completed in sequence, and provided information that was much more useful for promotional campaign planning. The factor analysis applied to the attitude and image batteries analysed the 400 informants in each of the surveys into eight distinct groups. Review of these groups, relating them to the marketing strategy, gave the opportunity for them to be revised and reduced into five segments. These were identified as 'interested in

European countries', 'Europhile', 'interested in culture', 'interested in leisure and sports', 'interested in scenery and the countryside' and 'interested in the food and wines of the country'.

The success of this analysis was effective for developing a series of themes for the promotional campaigns. On a regional basis this became even more effective, as the priority for promoting the region became more logical for the different segments in relation to the facilities and activities of that region.

Experience also shows that if sufficient segments are created, such as the five segments for the tourist office, a further cluster analysis is likely to make the age and socio-economic classification relate to the market, and help in using the data in strategic marketing planning. This was completed for the tourist office, and it allowed the socio-economic and age analysis to be clustered into six important groups. Relating the factor and cluster analysis created some very useful maps of the five market segments, giving the tourist office a clear analysis of the nature of the target tourist and who should be promoted to in terms of socio-economic targeting.

ANALYSIS THAT IS MARKET ORIENTED

The analysis of the data that is being collected should be thought about when planning the survey. It has a direct relationship with collecting interesting data and collecting information, which can guide the user to taking effective decisions, such as who to target with promotions. A basic analysis is likely to provide a 'look at the target', but is not going to be sufficiently informative about market trends or the attitude of the product or service user. Turning uninteresting computer tabulations showing columns of statistics into graphical pictures of the target customers through market maps makes the data more relevant to the market in reality.

Geodemographics and the application of the data in this analysis with data collected in a commissioned survey is the research industry's interpretation of 'virtual reality', making the statistics as realistic as possible in the context of the customer base. When the application of this technique allows better sales, marketing and communications targeting, the whole marketing process becomes more accurate.

Market mapping then allows the attitude and image of target customers to be related to market classification, and gives the manager a better opportunity to develop sales and marketing strategies that relate to their habits and lifestyles.

There are issues that managers need to understand about data analysis, which relate to ensuring that the data that has been analysed can be interpreted to its full potential. Our experience with managers who are not used to reviewing marketing data is that they need guidance on which of the data is representative and robust. Just as in Chapter 3 we talked about selecting a representative sample to interview, it is important to know what is representative and significant data when analysing computer tabulations.

First it is important to read all the data on a computer tabulation. Cross-tabulations are essentially simple to use, but they are key for understanding the results of research and examining market segments. They examine the responses to one question relative to the responses to one or more other questions, usually the data used to classify the survey. Each table sets out the answers to a question by the total sample, and by particular groups or subsets within the sample that are relevant to the aims of the research. Reading the table requires the analyst to read the numbers and percentages down each column, and then read the responses of different groups to compare them side by side for each part of the question.

The information on tabulations includes the following:

- Table and page number.
- Title. This is the question being analysed from the questionnaire.
- Base. This is the number of responses from the respondents who were asked the question. It is also possible that a subgroup has been selected to look at specific behaviour patterns.
- Rows. The listed answers to a question. It is good practice for the data analyser to list the options in the answer in descending order of the number of mentions.
- Columns. These are the variables that have been specified (such as age, income or sex, or number of employees, annual sales of a company) representing the subgroups that need to be compared.
- Content of the analysis. The most common form of content in the body of the computer analysis is to show the numbers of respondents that have answered and the percentage of the total or the subgroup total.

When an attitude or image statement-rating question is analysed, looking at the results of a five-point scale analysis, the computer analysing the data allocates a score to each positive answer and each negative answer. Any 'do not know' responses are excluded from the calculations. Multiplying the number of respondents by each score enables additional data to be printed on the computer table:

- Mean score. An arithmetic average within subgroups, and a measure of central location.
- Standard deviation. A measure of the average deviation of the sample from the mean.
- Standard error of the mean. An estimate of the standard deviation of the population from which the sample is drawn.
- Error variance. The square of the standard error, which is usually only required when calculating independent statistical T-tests (a test to see if two reported means are significantly different from each other) by hand.

Many statistics, spreadsheets and questionnaire packages, such as SNAP, QPS, Excel and SPSS, can generate cross-tabulations automatically. Analysis of cross-tabulations also facilitates data that can be presented in a variety of graphical formats using pie charts, line graphs, and bar charts.

Our experience with managers who are not familiar with reading computer tabulations is that they are concerned to know what is significant and representative data. This is important, as many of these people may not have the experience or time to complete statistical tests. Most want to talk about the findings in general terms; about the total market or customer base, not just the sample included in the survey. This is possible if the user of the data knows that the sample is representative of its population, but with any sample there is a chance that it may not be representative. As a result it is not possible to be certain that the findings apply to the total market.

The question then arises at what point or level of probability does a manager accept that the data is representative or not. The real significance level is the point at which the sample finding or statistic differs too much from the population expectation for it to have occurred by chance – the difference cannot be explained by random error or sampling variation and is accepted as a true statistical difference. At the 5 per cent significance level there is a 5 per cent probability, or a 1 in 20 chance, that the result has occurred by chance. This is the lowest acceptable level in market research.

An expert in these complex techniques should do detailed statistical testing. But a less experienced manager who wants reassurance about the data being reviewed on a computer table needs to understand how to check out how representative the data is. For example, it is important to look at the total sample size to ensure that it is large enough to calculate a percentage. If there are also sub-samples of small groups of respondents, or a small number of responses, a rule of thumb is to check to see if the sample base is 30 or more responses, as this is the lowest number that needs testing in statistical tests.

When looking at the results of a questionnaire on computer tables we also recommend another benchmark, to help to interpret the results: review the percentage of the responses for the proportion of answers to the question. If a response is less than 40 per cent it is important to check the sub-samples/market segments to see if there is an important minority that has agreed with that question. If a response is 40 per cent to 50 per cent to the question, then this can be interpreted as a good result and a firm or organization needs to consider the issues carefully. If it is an assessment of a new product or a check on the acceptance of a marketing strategy, then it is likely to be one to pursue, but it is likely to need a lot of marketing support and resources. If a response is between 50 per cent and 65 per cent to the question then this can be interpreted as an opportunity to go for, and is likely to be successful. If a response is 65 per cent or over to the question, then this is an opportunity to go for without question, particularly as it might be pursued by the competition and the research indicates that it will be very successful.

HINTS FOR MEASURING THE RESULTS

- Decide on the analysis at the research project planning stage.
- Where possible make the analysis meaningful and apply a statistical or analysis technique to your own results.
- Ensure that the data allows a manager to develop useful market segmentation, by analysing the data into the largest groups of consumers within the analysis.

- If a geodemographic analysis of the target market is completed it can have a direct effect on the structure and cost of any survey that is subsequently carried out. Knowing where the market is located, its size and profile can allow specific quota sampling to be used, which is more precise and cost effective.
- Spend time relating the attitude and behaviour of the target customer to the data to create a market map. Once the initial data analysis has been completed through a factor and cluster analysis, it is easy to create a map on a spreadsheet or graphics package on a PC.
- Whenever possible complete a graphical analysis of data. This allows fast and easy interpretation of segment analysis and consolidation of data for trends that exist in subsamples. What is important about this is that graphical analysis is more effective in communicating data to those who are not used to looking at it or interpreting it.
- Read computer tabulations carefully and interpret what is significant data, to conclude the relevant marketing actions.

5 You have the information – now use it

INTRODUCTION

Many managers think that when the research has been completed, the task of the research is finished. They have the information, they have read it and it should provide them with the answers they are looking for. But it is at this stage that many managers become dissatisfied, as they think that the information they have is not of use. Some managers even look at the research and feel it is not of interest to them, as it has not proved their own views. Many managers are also not sensitive to how to act on the implications of research, or do not have the right experience to do it. This situation should not occur if the research has been well planned and discussed with regard to the issues being evaluated. If it is carried out efficiently, with a questionnaire that covers all of the essential issues, and has a computer analysis that provides all of the results and detail of the information that has been collected, the research should provide the manager with all the information he or she needs.

A well-structured and informative project should enable a manager to use the information effectively. But when data is collected it is often presented without much thought and interpretation, and the key issues are not highlighted to the user. Reports are often prepared which mean much to those who have been directly involved in the project, but because they have been badly written, are ineffective as internal documents for other management. What is also very characteristic of many market research companies is that the reports lack detailed recommendations and implications – they do not cover all the issues that management should consider, discuss and implement. Often this is because the research companies are only information providers. The company is not sufficiently knowledgeable about the competitive decision making of interest to the research user.

Once the research has been completed it is essential that management recognizes there is a further stage of the project for deciding on the implications and using the decisions. Research becomes effective as guidance for setting objectives, developing strategies and implementing the right sales, marketing and communications methods. The skill in achieving this is to identify in a presentation or report the issues that have been confirmed.

A manager should recognize whether he or she has learnt anything new about the product, market or problem being researched. The data that does provide the new information, and which needs detailed thought and interpretation, should be highlighted for effective implementation. If there are any aspects of the information that are not clear and which need to be evaluated further, additional analysis of the data or additional research may need to be carried out to provide the essential information, as it could be that the questions that were designed for the research did not provide a useful analysis. It could be that the respondents have misunderstood the question, and therefore the answer is not relevant and cannot be used for good interpretation. Or it could be that the computer analysis is not detailed enough, and the real results of these questions are still hidden in the volume of data that has been collected.

Management needs to feel confident with the information it collects to use it effectively. It needs to recognize the positive and negative issues that emerge, and act on them appropriately. It also needs to realize that often a research project will highlight that certain issues need further research analysis. Although it may be that the managers have not asked the correct questions, this is likely to relate more to the fact that the research has been successful in identifying issues and problems that had not been known already. It is therefore logical to research these before taking any further decisions about them.

PRESENTING DATA EFFECTIVELY

The best way of reporting the data effectively is to verbally present the data before a report is written. The reasons for this relate to being able to understand the information that has been collected, and to being able to determine the initial implications of the research results. There are also a number of other benefits to making a presentation first:

- It assists in planning the extent of the interpretation: what is new information, what is old information and where similarities in the data have been identified. These similarities may relate to where certain types of respondents have made similar comments, or where the different types of respondent have a strong opinion about issues all through the research analysis.
- It helps to define whether the research objectives have been met and how successful the project has been in providing more information than had been expected. If the objectives have not been met it gives managers an opportunity to explain what problems occurred in the research and what implications exist as a result.
- It helps to identify any problems with the data, and if those seeing the data for the first time do not understand it, provides an opportunity for clarification or for further computer analysis before the detailed report is written.
- It establishes the issues that have been confirmed in the research, and when it comes to writing the report, helps the report writers compile a document in a format and style that is acceptable to the reader. This is important for some companies from the point of view of the jargon and language used by management.

The experience of the author with managers who have little knowledge and exposure to presentations is that they like to have all the data presented to them, but in a very simplified format. They like to be guided through the statistics and shown the argument for the interpretation;

how the implications relate to their research objectives and the decisions they have to take. They are hungry for the information, but eager to understand the implications quickly.

The technological developments in the use of graphics in recent years have enabled large amounts of data to be presented in the shortest possible time. The range of software programs that now exists has helped to improve the way in which the results of a research project can be presented and interpreted. It has removed the situation of non-analytical managers peering at slides with a forest of numbers. It now allows them to enjoy a presentation that has variety in the use of numbers, words, graphs and even pictures. The graphic delivery of research results has also helped research be seen, realized and applied by a wider range of managers than in the past. Our experience is that graphic presentation of data in PowerPoint ensures easy data analysis and interpretation.

When the presentation is finished the report can be prepared. This will focus on:

- the issues the management team agreed on during the presentation;
- the interpretation of any special analyses that had been agreed as worthwhile during the presentation;
- the production of a report that is acceptable and interesting to the management of the company.

The skill here is to note the type of emphasis, phraseology and stated use of the information mentioned by the management in the presentation, and to incorporate all of these in the report.

COMMUNICATING KEY RESULTS

Our experience is that it is best to get together the team that has worked on the research or other managers also interested in the results, and review each question in the research in a PowerPoint presentation. We tend to run the presentations in a workshop style, giving enough time to have a discussion about the issues that were important in deciding to do the research, what additional issues and questions emerged as the project and the questionnaire developed, and other thoughts that have resulted from discussions as the project has progressed. We then run through the data slide by slide, showing the key results compared with any cross-analysis of data that has been identified as significant for that particular question.

When trend analysis is being shown, the slide should compare as many previous years as possible, to help to identify the key trends that exist in the market. What is important in this is to review the graphical display of data and define what is a trend. A change positively or negatively is an obvious trend to identify, but we also discuss when there is no change, as this could be a more significant trend for reasons that relate to the market or the focus of the research.

It is also important to show the different market segments in the presentation – age, sex or income, or type of company, annual sales and so on – as it is possible to identify where there are strengths or weaknesses in different market segments, or conclude that there are opportunities in selling, marketing or communicating to specific customer types.

Discussing the data slide by slide gives the user management team opportunity to comment. 'That information is interesting – is it possible to look at this customer type in more detail?' 'We now realize that we should have looked at this aspect, or ask an additional question. Is it possible to do any further analysis that helps with this?' As the presentation progresses it is then effective to make notes on what additional analysis can be developed, and any issues that need to be emphasized in the report, thus helping to customize the analysis for the company using the research results. Our experience is that this is an effective approach, and often companies we work with ask us to give additional presentations. These presentations are either to other personnel in the company, such as the sales and customer service personnel, or to distributors, agents and customers.

CUSTOMIZING REPORTS

A market research report should be a management document, which does not just end up on the shelf for reference, but is used and referred to on a continual basis. One of our clients, with whom we have worked for 10 years on an annual retail store survey, keeps his annual survey of the market in his briefcase. He is a sales manager who deals with a wide range of contacts in the industry, in this instance the book publishing and retailing sector. The report provides a competitive analysis of the performance of his company in the trade sector, and he says that he uses the research project – his 'Bible' – to help develop the sales arguments in the meetings that he has with trade customers. Often he finds himself 'educating' the personnel in sales meetings, as they do not have as much information as he does on the market.

Many researchers believe that customizing research reports is difficult unless there is an ongoing relationship with the user of the research. Effectively, the researcher is saying that over a period of time he or she is getting used to what the research users want, and as a result, the researcher improves the way in which he/she writes the report. My belief is that this is rather a lazy way of preparing effective reports, as every report that is written should be customized to the reader and the company that has commissioned the research project. This depends on the researcher developing an effective relationship with the report user, finding out about the use of the report, its circulation and so on, then writing the report in the context of what has been learnt about how the research will be used. Researchers therefore need to focus on their knowledge of the market, their experience in assessing sales and marketing in the market, and giving advice to a company as to whether the current research is typical of the type of data collected, or is different because of issues that relate to the market, the company itself or the product being researched.

A good report that is customized for the reader, needs to have the following qualities:

- It needs to relate the research project to the current market situation and trends. This helps to make the findings of the research more relevant to the users, but particularly to those who are not directly involved in the project.
- It needs to explain which parts of the database have evaluated or answered issues originally laid out in the objectives of the project. This helps to relate how the findings of the research have proved or disproved a research hypothesis.
- It needs to summarize the positive findings so that they are brought to the attention of the reader to interpret and act on.
- It needs to summarize the negative findings so that the reader can decide what to do about them and take decisions, which make them more positive.
- It should have a summary of the main findings at the beginning of

the report, in a section which highlights the content of the report and is easily digested by the reader.

■ Separate from the summary, it should have a recommendations section which takes the key findings and changes them into:

- action for managers to take;
- issues managers might like to consider that relate to strategies and objectives they are involved with;
- the rationale for taking decisions based on the facts presented from the respondents in the survey, who are likely to be current or potential customers, users or buyers of the products or services made or offered by the company.

A good report is a short report. It is one that is written in the language of the potential reader: the jargon, terminology and industry-related information the reader is used to. It is one that reports all the findings of the research clearly, gives management feedback on the problems and issues being researched, and provides actions on which to take decisions.

IDENTIFYING RESEARCH IMPLICATIONS

The most interesting aspect of finishing a research project is reading the computer tables for the last time, reviewing the presentation slides, and checking that the report contains the best of the research findings. It is only at this point that the writer of the report is ready to decide on the implications and the recommendations that can be made. However, it is not the easiest part of the research and reporting process, and identifying the implications effectively depends on the consultancy skills of the researcher. Knowledge of the market and interpretation of the research findings in this context of market activity improve the recommendations that can be made.

The implications of the research project are only going to be relevant to the reader, and accepted and agreed with, if the writer of the research report has:

■ a clear understanding of the market or the product or service being offered to the market;
■ a good understanding of what the readers are looking for in the information that they have requested;

- the ability to turn information into actions and to argue the rationale for these actions;
- an understanding of what issues are involved in deciding on marketing, sales and communications strategies, and which aspects of the data in the report support the need for specifying these;
- an understanding of the significance of the results of the research and what these imply. Has the result of this research been typical or different from other similar research?

What research report writers sometimes fail to do is to break down the constituent parts of the research findings so that they relate to the most important aspects that concern the reader. It is vital that a research report discusses:

- the marketing implications, highlighting implications concerning decisions the reader needs to take on how to approach the market, and how to adopt the most effective competitive strategy for selling to the market;
- the sales implications, detailing the sales methods, the sales structure, and the positioning that the sales team ought to adopt to persuade customers and potential customers to buy the products or services;
- the communications implications: how the company will project its image to the market and how it will use the terminology of the market, as collected in the research, to develop the best themes, strap lines and promotional messages to communicate both the features and the benefits of the products or services being promoted.

The implications section of a report also ought to make reference to the company's sales, marketing and communications strategies compared with those of leading competitors. Without this a company cannot establish whether the research results indicate a better, worse or same competitive positioning.

A professional research report writer will also be in a position to indicate whether the research has covered all the relevant issues, whether the research needs to be completed again to explore certain issues in more detail, or whether new research needs to be designed, set up and run to explore issues that have been identified from the initial research project.

CASE STUDY

A chartered surveyor: using a structured approach to implement research findings

Take the example of an established firm of chartered surveyors. Traditionally a company concentrating on estate management and development, it had grown its residential and commercial property business and set up a specialist division to handle leisure and tourism developments. The company had not adopted any formal roles and marketing plan, but had depended on the property portfolio, advertising in key journals such as *Country Life*, and using public relations to the property journalists and leisure writers to maximize its communications effort.

As the boom in the property sector dwindled in the last recession, the company increasingly came under competitive pressure. For the first time it appointed a marketing director who realized that the company required a central coordinating function to develop the appropriate marketing methods for each of the divisions. The new director adopted a planning procedure and took the opportunity of using specialist marketing consultants to set up a strategic marketing plan. He also initiated a review of the corporate image of the company, as this area had fallen behind the competition.

The consultancy obtained immediate agreement that any planning should be based on the attitudes of existing and potential clients, and on an assessment of the services of the chartered surveyors in relation to its main competitors. A 'perception' survey was set up among a series of target groups for each of the various divisions – these included recent customers, lapsed customers, non-customers, intermediaries, financial journalists and even competitors.

In-depth, semi-structured qualitative (attitude type) interviews with 22 clients were carried out, as was structured qualitative research by sending self-completion questions to 30 property media journalists. Following these initial evaluations quantitative research was also completed among the main client base, consisting of 1,000 self-completion questionnaires – 255 of these were returned.

In the quantitative (large-scale statistical) phase of the project, the clients regarded the professional expertise of the company as high. The quality of the work was good and there was little criticism of standards. The level of services was considered to be on a par with other major competitors. The company was considered to have a high profile in leisure (the newest division), landed estates and upmarket residential, with a low profile in the commercial sector. It was also seen to be poor in communicating with its client base, with a third of the respondents saying that they were not aware that the firm had other divisions, apart from the one they used. The majority of the clients wanted a more proactive approach to their business from the surveyor.

In contrast, the survey among the journalists showed that the firm had the lowest profile of a comparable group in the press, indicating that the media had not appreciated the extent of the company and its operations.

In the quantitative phase, the clients were asked to rate the services of the company using attitude statements which were drawn up to help the respondent in the survey discriminate between the surveyor and its competitors. The firm's strengths are seen to be 'helpful staff', 'professionalism', 'personal service', 'confidentiality', and 'quality of work'.

The results of the perception survey highlighted that the firm of surveyors needed to improve:

- its image in the marketplace as being a more proactive company;
- its sales ability, by providing clients with a more creative approach to their requirements;
- the ability of the professional staff. A training programme was initiated to increase their awareness of marketing, and to improve their sales skills;
- its overall marketing approach. Its emphasis on PR had not proved effective, and it was clear that the company urgently needed to become more aggressive with its sales and marketing, improve its communications and become more 'competitive'.

The perception survey was useful, as it helped the company see itself as clients saw it, and to focus and target its sales and marketing more effectively. However, when the results were presented to senior managers they were concerned about its findings. Comments were made by the board of directors that included 'We cannot use this information as it disagrees with our view of the market', and 'Senior and middle management will find it difficult to interpret this information.' What essentially the board was saying was that it was not used to using and interpreting data. It was a sales-led company and managers were not analytical in their approach to decision making.

The consultants responded aggressively but professionally in demonstrating to the board that its ostrich-like approach would damage the firm's competitive position in the market. They said that rejection of the data would not allow the company to take decisions from its clients' viewpoint, and this could affect its overall competitive position. Their solution was to develop strategic planning sessions, which were designed to help the board and managers not only to understand the implications of the research, but also to undergo training in how to be more analytical and consider the clients' viewpoint.

Brainstorming sessions were held where groups of managers were asked to list out their decisions on how to implement the data, and to present their rationale for taking the decisions. The consultants undertook the same exercise, and both groups then analysed each other's lists for the strengths and weaknesses of the decisions taken. When these activities had been completed the board of the company agreed that it had been short-sighted in its original comments and recognized that it had invested in a research project that had been worthwhile, and which all management could make good use of. The research and its implications had had an effect on the culture of the company and its use of information.

It is clear that traditional reporting methods for research would have been limited in this instance. Working with the management to interpret and implement the research achieved both acceptance and use of the data. In effect the analysis helped to 'educate' the user of the data on what was confirmed in the research, and what was new that needed to be applied to its decision making as a result.

CONCLUSION

When research information is made available there is work to be done to make the data meaningful to the managers wanting to use it. It is important for management to become confident with the data so that it can learn new aspects about its customers.

A full presentation of the data before the report is written provides an opportunity to review the data and develop 'the database' on the implications of the data and on how the information will be used. It also provides a forum for bouncing ideas around and for doing further analysis to prove or disprove the issues being discussed.

The report on the research will include all the issues discussed at the research presentation. Because the issues have been discussed and debated, the report document represents the agreed research interpretation: the consensus view of the management team.

The implications help to specify the marketing methods and techniques, which will allow a company to grow by improving consumer targeting. They become the benchmark from which further research and analysis is completed. They also provide a standard against which the effectiveness of decisions taken can be monitored. In this way research becomes an effective tool for identifying where there are opportunities for growing the business. Once these are identified, it also becomes the monitoring mechanism of the potential growth areas, indicating whether they are providing new success or whether further financial, sales or marketing support is needed to make them successful.

HINTS FOR USING THE INFORMATION

- Present the findings of the research before reporting on it, as the presentation will help to check out the acceptability of the information and other issues that need further analysis.
- Use graphic and colour formats for the presentations, as they will enhance the fast delivery of a large amount of information, as well as help the audience to assimilate, understand and interpret the information effectively.
- Develop reports that are interesting, relevant to the user and contain implications that make the research not just a piece of information, but something that can be acted on.

- Ensure that reports are customized, and that they are structured, focused and include detailed recommendations that relate to the user of the data and the reader of the report.
- Highlight the strengths and weaknesses of the research findings so that managers can review the positives and negatives to help them to improve and enhance their decision making.
- Provide detailed interpretation and sufficient information on the implications of the data to make the collection of the data worthwhile, rather than recognizing it as just a piece of information.
- When analysing research take a step back and decide what you really do not know about your customers.
- Develop a series of questions that need to be answered and which the research analysis has to review carefully.
- Determine what measurements of competitive positioning and market are required so they can be extracted from the database.

6 Making sure that the customers are happy

INTRODUCTION

One of the most interesting global developments over the last 10 years has been the interest in getting the customer viewpoint to verify attitudes to products and services. With innovation occurring more quickly and products becoming uniform in different markets around the world, customer service has become the focal point of effective marketing and communications.

Customer care monitoring has been the key growth area of the market research sector in recent years. The reasons for this include:

- Market stagnation, with some sectors experiencing excess supply. Many companies are therefore keen to keep their customer base and satisfy their customers in a way that their competitors are not able to do.
- Higher consumer sophistication, leading to greater expectations for being satisfied, has developed the 'charter' culture for satisfaction.
- Increased management interest in total quality management (TQM), which takes care of the balance between the external and

internal consumer, and how good interaction between the two enhances good customer care.

■ Increasing interest in finding out from customers how well the organization is doing.

■ The annual 'report card' on organizational performance and whether it is better or worse than last year.

■ The development of database marketing and the need to check out the attitudes of regular customers, compared with those who buy products or use services on a more infrequent basis.

The US government also recognized that putting people first means ensuring that the Federal government provides the highest quality service possible to the American people. In 1993 President Clinton passed Executive Order 12862 to establish and implement customer service standards to guide the operations of the executive branch. The main reason for this was to carry out the principles of the National Performance Review. All executive departments and agencies providing significant services directly to the public were to:

provide those services in a manner that seeks to meet the customer service standard established and shall take the following actions:

■ Identify the customers who are, or should be, served by the agency;

■ Survey customers to determine the kind and quality of services they want and their level of satisfaction with existing services;

■ Post service standards and measure results against them;

■ Benchmark customer service performance against the best in business;

■ Survey front-line employees on barriers to, and ideas for, matching the best in business;

■ Provide customers with choices in both the sources of service and the means of delivery;

■ Make information, services, and complaint systems easily accessible; and provide means to address customer complaints.

This was not ordered just to collect information. By March 1994, each agency was required to report on its customer surveys to the President. As information about customer satisfaction became available, each agency was also required to use that information in judging the performance of agency management and in making resource allocations. Each agency was also required to publish a customer service plan including customer service standards and plans for customer surveys.

Our experience with this activity has been developing the customer satisfaction survey for the National Ocean Service Marine Chart Division over the last 10 years. Apart from developing feedback data and providing statistics in the public domain, the impact of completing the surveys has been to:

- provide a better focus on service standards;
- implement workshops and seminars to communicate survey results;
- design and distribute more information to users, including the data and information in NOS 'outreach' activities.

THE RATIONALE FOR CUSTOMER MONITORING

Some managers may feel that they know the 'pulse' of opinion of their customers. Regular visits from field sales staff; technical representatives or any staff member can keep the communications between the supplier and the customer clear, and identify the strengths and weaknesses of the relationship. But this type of contact is not systematic in terms of an independent way of collecting information, and it is prone to bias. Individuals are always interested in presenting the positive aspects of business relationships, and any concern or dissatisfaction expressed by a customer is likely to be rationalized when reported back to senior management.

Independent objective customer analysis will provide meaningful feedback, which can be tracked through trend analyses over time. Some companies that have regular research activities may believe that they are already collecting sufficient customer monitoring information through their survey research and customer research. But this is not quite the same as the specific role of customer care, as it is important to construct a questionnaire that addresses two areas relating to the relationship with customers. Indeed, there is also a potential for confusion between general survey data and the customer care analysis, and specific customer monitoring has to be planned, set up and analysed as a separate activity. The two areas that are effective for a customer care programme, are, first, assessing all elements of contact with the company: letters received, telephone contact, speed of dealing with enquiries, speed of delivery, overall customer service and so on; and second, giving an evaluation of whether customers believe the company has provided a good or bad product and service, and the degree to which they have been satisfied with the type of service provided.

An efficient and effective way of completing this analysis is to create attitude statements that describe the type of contact the customer may have had. 'Fast and efficient response to enquiries', 'clear invoicing', 'solved my query very quickly' and 'answered the phone quickly' are all typical statements which the informants in the survey are asked to rate according to a bipolar scale from Agree to Disagree. The overall assessment is taken from a question about satisfaction levels: 'Overall how satisfied are you with the service provided by....'? Again this is rated on a bipolar scale from Very Satisfied to Very Unsatisfied.

Where there is overlap between a customer monitoring programme and regular survey research, there is the need to link the findings of the assessments of service and overall satisfaction with what is important or unimportant to the customer in relation to how the service is provided. There is nothing wrong with this, but it has to be taken as a rating in conjunction with the customer ratings, rather than completed as a rating in isolation.

USES FOR CUSTOMER CARE MONITORING

Management now has the opportunity of taking advantage of a series of new trends that have emerged for customer monitoring. These include:

- The focus on researching customer retention, making sure customers are as satisfied as before.
- The growth of 'mystery shopping': observation of how customers are cared for (the virtual reality of customer monitoring) at the place of work as well as how the process of dealing with customers is completed.
- Using the data results to provide an index which, if collected regularly, provides an indication of performance which all management can use as an indicator of the quality of their decision making.
- Calculating staff rewards and profit sharing based on the performance indices collected from customers as the measure of success or failure.

- Reporting customer care monitoring results in companies' annual reports, newsletters or monthly bulletins.
- Using the research findings on a regular basis to check whether sales, marketing or communications plans are achieving the goals agreed and set as annual tasks.

There has also been a consolidation of an increasing trend in creating data where it did not already exist, but its contribution is to provide an additional indication of how effectively service is provided. Publishers researching bookshops' customers, and industrial manufacturers researching the end-user market of the product that their components constitute, are both forms of customer care. It is getting good feedback from the user on how well the user is being looked after, and whether you are achieving this more effectively than your competition.

Customer care research is therefore an important technique for measuring performance, evaluating people and services, and the style of service that is offered. It evaluates all aspects of service and how it is provided, such as standing in a line, and the way in which the service is delivered, such as the friendliness and courtesy of staff.

KEY GUIDELINES

Our experience is that management needs to be aware of key guidelines when making sure that customers are happy. These include:

- Obtain the commitment for all staff and management to collect, interpret and use the data, as it is essentially data about how well they are doing.
- Accept that a performance indicator is the focal point of the quality management programme, which 'drives' the customer monitoring.
- Plan carefully the questionnaire content and the specialist techniques for the data collection so that they are sensitive to all customer case issues.
- Analyse the data graphically so that the findings, trends and implications can be realized and interpreted quickly.
- Recognize that the trends that are identified may lead to a restructuring or redesigning of the project and questionnaire content, as

management realizes the need for more precise feedback from customers, depending on how they view performance.

▪ Accept that these research studies should be done on a regular basis. Many customer care research programmes are not effective unless they are completed over a three-year period, the minimum that is effective for identifying trends and discussing their impact on the company, its systems and the decisions that it has been taking.

CASE STUDY

A US airline: using research to provide an integrated monitoring system

Let us take the example of an international US airline, which has developed the results of the customer care research into the corporate culture of the whole company. Delivery of bags at the carousel at the airport, waiting time for take-off on the runway, reaching the gate on arrival at the destination airport, and schedule reliability are all presented monthly from the continuous customer satisfaction surveys. Competitive and internal on-board survey results are even presented to flight crews so that actionable market research is used by operating staff, financial staff and marketing staff to check how well the overall service is being received.

Decision makers are therefore involved in customer attitudinal data by seeing continuous data on customer attitudes. What is interesting about this airline is how it uses the data for quantifying trends. Typical management meetings of any company include viewing management financial data and hearing a manager say, 'We are 5 per cent above the revenue plan'. Now companies can add other comments, as this airline does: 'Customer comments on our schedule reliability are five points above our goal.'

However, a company like this airline, which is customer-led in its decision making, has to distribute the information through the company carefully. The airline has created measurement techniques to make the 'intangible aspects of its service into tangibles'.

The data extracted from on-board surveys is sampled in various languages. The surveys are run with two questionnaires. One asks about marketing topics: issues like ticket purchase decision, timing of travel and where the ticket was purchased, length of stay, the purpose of the trip, awareness of flight schedules, fares and so on. The other questionnaire is concerned with customer satisfaction. Passengers are asked to rate all aspects of the operation from reservations and flight check-in to on-board service and meals service. One per cent of flights are sampled within the United States and 10 per cent internationally. Passengers have been asked to give their names and addresses. The zip code analysis is used with a geodemographic package, which provides segmentation, and demographic data as discussed earlier in the book.

This customer monitor has become very effective for quantifying the importance of different areas of the airline's operation by using factor and discriminant analysis of all the attributes and the degree to which they explain a customer's flight satisfaction. The airline has found that its customer satisfaction research has become more central to the business planning than other aspects of its marketing. This is because the management style is goal driven and is open to accepting and using quantified data.

CASE STUDY

The leading US distributor of maps and guides to all retail outlets selling these products

Another good example of customer care monitoring is from a company based in Santa Barbara, California. It is the leading US distributor of maps and guides to all retail outlets selling the products. The company over a period of years had built up a reputation for advising the companies it worked with on what they should stock and sell to their customers, how the stock should be presented and which were the new and leading products. Its retail customers depended on the knowledge of the company and its staff, and as a result the distributor had to increase the number of customer service personnel, to take calls from retailers during retail sales hours.

The author's company completed an annual survey on the consumer market for maps and guides, and as a result of this the distributor asked for the data to be classified by all the leading retail outlets for maps and guides, so that customer service could advise the different outlets on which products customers had been buying in their stores, which they were interested in buying and what could sell well. This process was developed over two years, and the data presented to all of the distributor's customer service, procurement and vendor management staff. As a result of this a customer service measure was set up to add to the annual presentation, an annual 'report card' on the standard of customer service it was providing.

This was developed further over another two-year period and the customer service measures set for a trend analysis. The results of the research showed customer service to be very high in the view of the retail customers, and that the reputation of the company and its ability to provide good information were the key attributes of the service.

The distributor decided that the results of the research indicated that the company needed to be providing as much information as possible to its customers, either via its customer service staff or through other communications. Many of its customers used the customer service team as a help line, to call up and get advice on what products to stock, what was new, and whether there were recommendations based on the experience of other customers. So the company developed a regular programme of looking at the research data and referring to it when customer information calls were taken by the customer service team. It published regular newsletters and mailers, to help to provide as much information as possible. The second year of the customer service assessment showed that this had been effective in the relationship between distributor and the buyers at the retailers. In the second survey the distributor placed some questions on the questionnaire that were designed to ask the retailers what additional services or products they would like the distributor to supply. The retailers indicated that four of the six ideas the distributor had were of interest to them. So future surveys, apart from continuing to monitor overall satisfaction, will also measure satisfaction with the four new services provided.

ASSESSING THE IMPACT OF THE RESULTS

Customer care monitoring is widely used by management, and in many companies has involved those who have not completed research activities before in detailed and complex projects. Experience shows that it is essential to review the data carefully, as many managers have felt that after two to three years few changes in the data indicates that it may not be worthwhile continuing with similar research in the future.

Little change in the data year on year could be an important check on the strengths of a company competitively, and continuing to monitor customer attitudes on this basis needs to be interpreted as a success story, rather than a problem. But it is important to a company to see this type of information, as any small change could create a focus on that part of the customer support, which if changed could have an important effect on customer attitudes. An analysis such as this has also had the effect of changing the nature of the study in the future, to provide more detail and feedback. A typical action has been to segment the customer base into more target groups, so that the analysis searches the attitudes of different customer types more sensitively. The result of doing this has been to focus more on the support that can be given to different customer types.

CONCLUSION

Customer care monitoring is developing and changing. Companies have become more interested in collecting data on customer retention and on customers who have lapsed. Companies have developed it to understand how new customers' expectations are satisfied. In the future there will also be a greater dependence on relating the findings of the research to all elements of company operations. It will therefore help to assess how to improve market penetration, market shares, and the overall sales of the company.

A report from the Henley Centre and the Chartered Institute of Marketing stated:

This more competitive environment will focus greater attention on the potential of existing customers. This will take the form of:

- Assessing lifetime values and thus the value of promoting loyalty
- The ways of increasing the value of given customers through cross selling
- Identifying which customers provide the fastest, most cost effective and rewarding results on the investment of resources.

It is therefore extremely important that the marketing of a company is directed towards building loyalty among existing customers as the cost of replacing an existing customer with a new one can often be as high as tenfold.

In order to measure the success of the customer loyalty it is essential that trading and evaluation procedures are incorporated. Marketing needs to be monitored against objectives set by measuring changes in behaviour and attitude. The results of the tracking provide clear performance measures and information for future planning.

Customer monitoring programmes are making the techniques of survey research much more accessible to all levels of management – as high as boards of organizations. They are exposing more managers to the analysis, interpretation and effects of using external independent data. Management is therefore finding that new company systems are being created which help it to take customer-led decisions. Later in the book we will see the significance of trend analyses, and how they impose on the long-term decisions that management take.

Trend analysis of customer monitoring programmes really does provide feedback on whether the right decisions are being taken. Good interpretation of these programmes proves that data can be used to ensure sales increase. The task is to listen more to customers, check how satisfied they are, and focus services on their needs.

HINTS ON DEVELOPING CUSTOMER MONITORING

- Gain agreement with all levels of management that customer monitoring feedback is to be used at management meetings to measure performance.
- Decide on the techniques to be used, but ensure that sufficient numbers of interviews are carried out to represent all types or classifications of customers.
- Use a definitive list of customers, which provides for both users and buyers of your products and services to get a good comparison of the type of customer and the contact he/she has with the company.
- Design the attitude statements carefully to measure all aspects of customer contact. Do not make the evaluation too exhaustive, but ensure it includes all aspects that can be assessed for good and bad performance.
- When you first set up the programme, design it bearing in mind what has to be assessed and measured in a 'trend' analysis.
- Develop your 'benchmarks' to measure success or failure.
- Keep the analysis of the information simple, using graphic output so that the data can be used widely in the company.
- Decide on the feedback to the customers of the results of the customer monitoring. Publishing data in the annual report, newsletters and other company information is an important way of reassuring present customers about, and demonstrating to potential customers, the quality and level of service.
- As customer-monitoring progresses, add in questions to customers about ways in which services can be changed, improved or developed. When these are analysed, add these to the annual assessment to ensure that they are monitored along with the existing established measures.

7 Tracking trends and changing decisions

INTRODUCTION

So far in this book we have seen how to make good decisions by recognizing that using information enhances the decision making process. We have also established what is essential information to a manager, both data that is available from internal systems and data that can be collected from desk research. There is in addition a series of external research techniques, which are more desirable to use because they yield good information that relates to sales, marketing and communications. We have realized, too, that there are important ways of analysing, presenting and reporting the data that make the research findings both actionable and effective.

It is also important for management to understand how to work with these techniques to make use of research-led sales, marketing and communications in decision making. Effective research use and implementation have a direct relationship with being able to devise ways of setting strategies to expand company business. Those who have experienced the effective use of information to grow business have realized that it is not the research they have been doing, but the way they have been doing it that has resulted in making sure the research is effective. The key is to be able to use research to:

- track trends, to get the total picture of the market;
- understand changes in the market;
- learn to review and change decisions based on the trends that have been identified.

Research can often be viewed as providing information as a 'snapshot' of customers' opinions and the situation in the market. If a series of snapshots are created through the research being completed on a regular basis, then the snapshots can be linked together and the findings of each stage interpreted. In fact it is just like creating a movie, with the frames of each 'take' or 'snapshot' providing a sequence, which can be interpreted by management to monitor the effectiveness of the decisions it has taken between intervals. Unlike a movie, the sequence of the research may not have an ending or conclusion, as it provides an ongoing view of the situation. The epic effect of the trend monitoring may have a direct influence on the nature of the decisions management takes over a long period of time, because of the trends that are likely to emerge.

Management may also find that a practical and effective application of research techniques is to track trends in the delivery of customer service, as we have seen in the previous chapter. In the last 10 years there has been an increase in the number of management teams using research in this way, which in itself is exposing traditional research techniques to higher levels of management in the company. Senior management are now more concerned about customer satisfaction, and they are becoming more involved in designing research projects that are providing the benchmark data for customer monitors that will last over a period of many years.

Using research information to track trends is likely to have a direct effect on increasing sales and growing the business. Understanding, tracking and monitoring your own company's successes, failures, competitive positions, new products or communications on a continuous basis will give an independent and objective way of improving decision making. If the analysis is used by all levels of management in a company, then it is not just using research as a management tool, it is proving that research can be used as the most fundamental way of developing, running and implementing sales and marketing plans.

MONITORING MARKET SHARES

Most companies are proficient in monitoring market share, but few use research techniques in a systematic manner. Share monitoring is effective and is vital in:

- understanding if your sales are better in an increasing market, a static market or a declining market;
- knowing which competitors are performing better and which are worse;
- knowing which product categories are selling better or worse than those of your competitors;
- identifying whether your own awareness in the market is better or worse than that of your competitors;
- establishing if sales are particularly concentrated in a customer base, compared with competitors' sales concentration;
- checking out if your sales and promotional targeting is effective.

Market share monitoring differs in both industries and individual companies. Each method needs to be discussed to determine how effective it is for growing business. The methods available are discussed below.

Informal discussion and information exchange with competitors to check how the company is performing compared with them

This is typically done at trade shows and exhibitions. It is a very unsystematic way of collecting market share data. It is also likely to be inaccurate, depending as it does on estimates and indicators that are verbal hearsay, and in some instances on figures that one company may want its competitors to believe but that may not reflect the real situation.

Submitting data to a trade association or an independent organization appointed by a group of companies in the same industry or sector to collect and disseminate the information collected

This is a systematic method for collecting market share data, and it is a way for competing companies, sensitive about using data with competitors' information, to become more analytical in their approach to decision making. As a method for sharing sales information it has to include the following:

- Careful preparation of the questionnaire or a data sheet that is used to collect the information. It must have classifications for market and product sectors or categories, which are used by or meaningful to each company carrying out the information exchange and share analysis. This has to be developed, discussed and agreed as it is unlikely that each company will have the same classifications.
- The sales periods of the data being submitted must be the same for each company, otherwise there cannot be an effective comparison of the information.
- The analysis must also be informative and provide information that can easily be interpreted.
- The market share calculations are documented so that all parties using them know how they are calculated.

Some market share information exchanges just take in the data from all companies and then disseminate it without any further analysis. Say, for example, 54 insurance companies submit their monthly sales data for life insurance policies. These are listed in 23 different categories. The 54 entries are added for each of the 23 categories and the data printed on separate sheets. Twenty-three sheets are then issued showing entries numbered 1 to 54, the numbers being the only identity given to the companies participating in this data exchange. Each company therefore gets back their own sales data and those of competitors, but only in the context of the sales trends in the product category.

Market share monitoring has become much easier as databases and spreadsheets have become the basic tool of management information systems on PCs. It also has changed some management's attitudes to how quickly it needs data and how current the information should be. Sophisticated market share systems in the food and drink retailing sectors, automotive and automotive parts distribution sector, computer hardware and software sales are now set to provide information on a weekly basis. This requires dedicated staff to both input and output the data. The volume of information that is generated is often too much and too detailed for a typically busy manager to read, interpret and act on. Most of this type of information is now not printed on computer output or spreadsheet tables, but in a graphic format, which allows the quick interpretation of overall trends. This is more useful for a busy manager, as it improves his or her ability to be able to take decisions fast.

DEVELOPING TRACKING STUDIES

Earlier in the book we discussed the need for developing customer data to gain an understanding of the customer profile: where customers are located and how their needs change. Tracking studies are essentially a means of collecting this customer data on a continuous basis. They are effective for monitoring all the sales, marketing or communications that companies are planning, have in progress or have completed.

Typically there are two types of tracking study which are used effectively by companies. One is a study that concentrates on the marketing effects of a communications campaign. Used mainly by companies that have heavy expenditure in advertising and promotions, data from these studies provide feedback on the effectiveness of the promotions in the total market. The traditional approach to this type of tracking study is to divide it into at least three stages. The initial stage is the 'pre-campaign' stage, which should include all the questions that the company has to ask to benchmark the trends in the tracking study. Benchmarking means asking the questions in this initial phase and then repeating the same questions in the subsequent phases to identify the changes.

The 'pre-campaign' stage needs to establish what is the market that the communications usually reaches, what is the awareness level of the company investing in the communications, how this awareness level relates to that of competitors, and what recall exists for any communications. As this phase of the research typically takes place before a communications campaign is initiated, the data will provide good information on all of the above except for recall of the communications.

What is important, and is sometimes forgotten, is the need to analyse this benchmark data to interpret it and understand the implications of what it is saying. The reason for this is to make the research effective, and understand the market's attitudes and reactions to the upcoming communications, so they can be used effectively.

Analysis of this initial phase is likely to help to define questions that could be added to the subsequent phases. Failure to complete this analysis at the first stage could mean that later stages do not contain the right question content, which helps to collect data on whether company communications are causing target consumers to react or change their attitudes.

The second and any subsequent stages, phased in when communications are transmitted to the current and/or the potential market, should include the original stage one questions; otherwise the changes, drift and trends cannot be monitored. However, additional questions should be added to allow for sufficient evaluation of the effects of the communications. It is particularly important to assess the visuals of the communications to identify what is liked and disliked. Equally, information on the content, the copy or the words, the slogan or jingles and the strap lines is going to provide a better understanding of whether the communications are consumer oriented and effective from the point of view of obtaining customer loyalty and increasing sales.

The second type of tracking study, which is essentially to gain understanding of the users and buyers and their needs and buying requirements, needs to be on a regular basis. 'Regular' has to be defined according to the dynamics of the market sector in which the reader's own products and services exist. The food, financial services and publishing sectors need such a study annually. Printing machinery, agricultural machinery or any 'minority' market is likely only to need data every other year. The computer sector needs it quarterly or every two months. However, the content of this type of tracking study ought to be specified carefully. The structure of the questions should be reviewed in the context of the reader's own product group and industry structure. The questions should relate to the following headings:

- Classification of the market. In consumer markets this should be age, sex, social class, income and any other factors that are important for classifying the market, such as leisure and lifestyle factors. In industrial markets this should be type of company, turnover, profitability, number of employees and any other characteristics that need to be classified.
- Definition of owners and non-owners, users and non-users, and how these target markets classify into 'heavy' or very regular users or buyers, 'medium' or fairly frequent users or buyers, and 'light', infrequent users or buyers.

- How much is paid for the products or services.
- How much is bought/used of the products or services.
- Where the products or services are bought or used, and where buyers/users prefer to buy or use the products and services.
- Attitudes to the products or services (rated by attitude statements, phrased in the context of factors important to consumers, or how they tend to buy or decide to buy products).
- Media used to promote products or services.

Then the questionnaire should carry any other questions relating to new product development, and of course the communications development, and the communications campaign being evaluated. This is also another area where a badly designed questionnaire will not give the best feedback. Many managers forget to explore the reasons for the opinions given, and it is these that provide the key to establishing whether a communications strategy needs to be refocused, or elements of it changed or improved.

The following provides the guidelines to what should be included in the communications section of the questionnaire:

- awareness of the company, product or service (unprompted);
- awareness of the campaign (unprompted);
- awareness of the company, product or service (prompted);
- awareness of the campaign (prompted);
- what is liked about the campaign and why;
- what is disliked about the campaign and why;
- what is liked about the theme and why;
- what is disliked about the theme and why.

If the communication medium is a newspaper advertisement:

- what is recalled about the copy of the advertisement;
- how the advertisement caused the person seeing it to change his/her attitude towards the company, product or service.

If the communication medium is a television or radio advertisement:

- what was liked or disliked about the visual or audio part of the campaign;

- what was liked or disliked about the 'jingle', voiceover and content of the advertisement;
- how the advertisement caused the person seeing it to change his/her attitude towards the company, products or service.

Analysis of all this information will not only identify the successes and failures of a communications campaign, it will also help to focus on where future campaigns can relate more specifically to the target market. Increasing the target market will, of course, lead to a growth in business.

USING KEY DATA TO TAKE DECISIONS

The research sector is full of technical experts, academics and practitioners who are very keen to talk about how research is done and what are the technical strengths and weaknesses of the research. It is important to use this 'focus of excellence' to ensure that the research helps decision making. As there are so many techniques available, it is sometimes difficult to decide which to use.

Managers who are somewhat confused about the plethora of advice and guidance available need to organize themselves to know what to use. Earlier in the book we mentioned managers who do not think research is of any use to them, because they have not thought about or discussed with colleagues what information is needed. The key to using data to take decisions is to list:

- facts that you know about the market or the customers, which you need corroborated or confirmed as issues which then are not likely to be disputed or evaluated any further;
- information that you recognize you do not have or data that clearly will help to take decisions which have not been taken because of uncertainty;
- ideas that need to be tested out and which will provide the research user with information which will reduce risk and the uncertainty of launching a new product or service which may not have been tested before.

Experience shows that managers who do this benefit from thinking through systematically what data they could use. Most of them recognize that they have a vast amount of experience, preconceptions and prejudices, but few hard facts on which to base customer-led decisions. The result of this can be summarized into a number of different sets of data, which become more central to the decision making process. They are:

- statistics on the size of the market and the strata sizes within the sector;
- data on the structure of the market in the context of suppliers and user industries;
- information on the market trends and how they relate to products and services already in the market;
- statistics on the share of the market the company commands and how this relates to competitors' shares;
- user, buyer and potential customer data on the image of the company;
- independent assessment of marketing methods used by the company and how competitors' methods differ;
- independent assessment of the sales methods and an evaluation of their effectiveness;
- information on the effectiveness of distribution methods and how to stimulate them to achieve greater effectiveness;
- customer assessment of the acceptability of product shipment and packaging;
- statistics on the profitability of the product portfolio;
- statistics on costs and pricing;
- customer assessment of the products and what they like and dislike about them;
- customer evaluation of the effectiveness of the services of the company;
- use, storage, dissemination of industry data and how this adds to the intelligence of the company;
- statistics on non-domestic markets for all of the above and how similar they are to, or different from, the domestic market;
- survey research information on reaction to new products and product concepts being developed;
- systematic analysis through survey research of competitive activity;
- customer data on the demand for products;
- regular survey research data on users' attitudes and behaviour, and assessment of the image of the company.

Managers who only understand marketing as the selling function staff many organizations at a high level. They are concerned with the optimum price for the product they make with the most cost effective production. Data such as the 19 points listed above tends not to feature in their day to day decision making. Reviewing this list will clearly show that their decisions are not market-led and comparative to other suppliers. The most important aspect they lack is the monitoring technique and advantage of using market research effectively.

CASE STUDY

A food casing company: using research to track trends

Tracking trends depends on the product and the market and the structure and characteristics of that market. The food casing sector provides a good example of why trend information becomes not just essential in understanding how to grow business, but important in knowing how to respond to overall marketing activity.

Food casings are supplied to food manufacturers to make the end product. Food casing manufacturers are therefore dependent on the success of the sales and marketing activity of the food manufacturer. Indeed, they are essentially removed from the real consumer: the buyer of the end product that is made up from all the food and casings.

Concerned about forecasting the market to maintain good customer relations for existing customers, and also to devise ways in which to develop and increase the market, a food casing supplier decided to set up and run a market research programme. The company's rationale for doing this was to 'get closer' to the market to examine the trends and market characteristics of the end-user market, as this has a direct impact on how the manufacturer can maintain and increase sales. The sales and marketing management realized that it could not make market-led decisions without any independent data, which could help the company to convince its customers about consumer preference for its products, and also identify emerging trends in the market. What was interesting about this company was its concern to develop a programme which could be updated regularly and which could provide an 'early warning' system by tracking trends, and an effective monitoring system to measure the effects of the decisions taken. The marketing information system that was created by this company included the following.

Analysing the company's sales statistics to determine market performance

Three years' data was analysed in the computer and a trend analysis created. New sales statistics were then added to this annually and a monitoring system was created. The company wanted to use this data as a predictor of market performance. The sales force had estimates of competitors' sales, and these were added into the computer analysis. Additional data on economic growth and other market influences were also included and a 'market model' was created.

Developing annual survey research, identifying consumer preferences for the company's products versus competitors' products

Regular product tests were completed to track consumer preferences for the food casings, compared with competitors' products. This data was analysed and prepared in a graphic format, which showed simply the percentage of consumers in the market that preferred the casings to competitors' products. This information was given to the sales representatives so that it could be shown to customers and potential customers as objective, independent data proving why the product should be bought and used to manufacture the end product. As it was tracked over a period of time, the data became even more convincing in demonstrating customer loyalty and product performance compared with varying competitor product quality.

Setting up a user and attitude survey, which was then repeated every other year among a representative sample of the population of consumers in the total market

This research project included all elements of market analysis and consumer classification. It was designed to provide all the background information on users and buyers of the end-products, which included the food casings. The data covered trends in the size of the market, the number of consumers paying for the product and how much they paid. It also gave a competitive overview of which end-user products were bought, who was buying them and an evaluation of consumer attitudes to products that were introduced to the market. The data was also analysed in a graphic format and used in discussions with customers and for presentations at customer conferences. This provided the company's customers with more detailed knowledge of their own customers – consumers – which helped both the casing supplier and food manufacturers to understand market trends and customers' needs more clearly.

Research for this company was not just about providing essential information for market and product planning. It became the means of convincing customers that it had a good knowledge of the market. This also allowed the casing supplier to use independent and objective data to persuade customers to buy its products, and thus helped the company directly to grow its business. It was also using independent objective consumer data – product users and buyers – to inform its own customers, the sausage manufacturers and the retailers, on what opportunities existed to grow the market, and as a result their business.

This company had been running this programme for nine years, and has researched European and Asia Pacific markets annually. The more research the company completed, the more it realized that it had more information on its customers than its own customers had. As a result of this the company presented the data to agents and sales personnel in the different markets, the trading manufacturers and where possible the trading retailers. The company's investment in the research was improving the whole sector's knowledge and helping suppliers, manufacturers and retailers to get closer to their customers.

DEVELOPING TREND DATA

Research is not worthwhile unless it makes a contribution to decision making. Its contribution comes when it provides new and additional data that influence management thinking.

Involvement in research is the manager's chance to play a role, just as a writer of a play or a movie script has to define the roles of actors. The writer will decide on the theme or purpose of the movie. Characters are created to communicate the writer's message. The plot will test out the theme and the purpose, with scenes that build up the overall picture of the underlying reason for the script. Taken together, in sequence, the scenes form a logical delivery of the movie and allow the person watching to learn something. The moviegoer will leave the theatre or the movie understanding a subject in more detail.

Research fulfils the same function for the manager as a play or a movie for the scriptwriter. The manager has to set out the theme or purpose of doing the research. The information requirements that he or she defines are likely to prove or disprove this theme, depending on the answers of those interviewed. The questionnaire, if constructed carefully, in sections that relate to various aspects of the overall purpose, will help to build a picture of the issues that relate to the theme. The analysis, presentation and reporting of the data will help the managers to understand what they have learnt from the research.

The important point for a manager to realize is that if the above is achieved then, just as a movie, there is a beginning, middle and an end to a research project. But a movie with frames missing is disjointed and is unable to communicate the theme effectively – the viewer will not know the whole plot and will not realize the sequence of the message.

A research project is similar to this. Unless the research is planned over a series of projects relating to the market, the results are unlikely to deliver the right message. It is therefore important to develop trend data, to understand the overall implications of decision making and use the trend information that is emerging to influence and eventually direct decision making.

The benefit of developing trend information is to create a real and detailed understanding of the company, its products and services in the market, its competitive positioning, and to monitor the effectiveness of its sales, marketing and communications. None of these are going to be appreciated if research is completed on an ad hoc 'one off' basis. The snapshot is like one frame of the movie – it only gives an impression of the theme, the situation of the plot, and part of the communications at one particular time.

Companies who have realized the benefits of trend data say that:

- The trends give them a better long-term perspective of the decisions they have taken, helping to focus on the key decisions for the future.
- It is easier to monitor the reactions of the target market and identify more clearly where improved targeting is needed.
- Information on the effectiveness of the sales, marketing and communications strategies over a long period helps managers to allocate funds more effectively to sales, marketing and communications departments.
- The research becomes a better investment as it becomes the monitoring tool and is the 'early warning system' for making corrective competitive action or identifying new market or product opportunities.
- The research highlights when additional 'problem solving' or 'issue evaluating' information is needed, and also makes its contribution in helping to design more relevant and more specific ad hoc research.

Trend data helps managers to monitor market sizes and the performance of the company in the marketplace. Regular use of attitude and image statements in attitude and image batteries that are not changed over the long period of the research provides the means of monitoring the total presence of the company in the market, and a basis for the marketing actions that are required. The sensitivity of these statements is so precise in monitoring attitudes; motivations and buying habits that long-term customer monitoring programmes depend on the effectiveness of this technique. Trend data therefore gives the company total performance feedback, establishing whether management is taking the most effective decisions to ensure that the company grows.

IDENTIFYING COMPETITIVE POSITIONING

As markets have become more competitive and as businesses have become more pressured to meet changing customer needs, there has been an increasing need to be ahead of competitors. But many companies do not systematically analyse competitor activity, and they have been getting more and more assistance in collecting this information. Many companies take informal approaches such as:

- discussing competitor activity at management meetings, but only using general knowledge of competitors, rather than reviewing specific data;
- collecting information from distributors and customers in informal discussions and using this as feedback on how competitors are satisfying customers;
- getting listed on competitors' databases in order to be mailed their catalogues, mailers and other information – but of course to a home address!

It is becoming increasingly characteristic to develop marketing surveys and customer satisfaction surveys with questions that address competitors, to make the comparisons in the data collected. Our experience is that many managers do not think about doing this in their surveys, and that when this information is obtained, senior management in a company tend to view the research results more positively. When added to surveys on a regular basis, the data provides important feedback to help managers know their company's own strengths and weaknesses, and where resources should be allocated.

The technique to develop this information is to add the following types of questions, but ensuring that attitude statements are used, to get as independent assessment as possible from respondents. The questionnaire needs to have questions that allow for a general analysis of all suppliers in the market, and specific questions on the image of the suppliers, as follows:

- Which of the following suppliers are you aware of (unprompted)?
- Which of the following suppliers are you aware of (prompted)?
- Many users of these companies in this sector have made comments about what is important to them in assessing the services of the suppliers. Which of the following are important to you, and please tell me how important by using the scale Very important, Important, Neither important nor unimportant, Unimportant, or Very unimportant. The attitude statements could include the following:
  - fast response to requests;
  - good at providing information;

- regular visits from sales staff;
- regular visits from technical staff;
- have an innovative approach to product development.

▪ I would now like to ask you about each of the suppliers you have said you know. Please tell me how satisfied you are with the services that each provides using the scale Very satisfied, Satisfied, Neither satisfied nor unsatisfied, Unsatisfied or Very unsatisfied. A grid is then developed for each supplier listed, and respondents are asked to rate each supplier for the aspects covered in the list of attitude statements above.

Analysis of this data requires many computer tabulations and comparative PowerPoint slides to show the customers' attitudes to each company and to identify where there are similarities and differences. If the study is updating previous data then many slides are needed, as the additional analysis has to be the year-to-year trends, to see how the long-term picture influences decisions.

CONCLUSION

Market research is a marketing tool and management discipline, which is underestimated for its contribution to decision making. Improving knowledge of the market will help to anticipate market or customer needs and allow the company to react before any changes occur to these in the normal course of business. By monitoring the effectiveness of the marketing methods used and evaluating them over a long period of time, research makes a definitive contribution to the decision making process.

Regular and effective feedback, providing good knowledge and information, has to have a priority over guesstimating and assuming without the relevant facts. Data and information help a manager to get closer to the market and understand why a customer wants a product, what influences the customer to buy it, and how much the customer is prepared to pay. Knowing this from independent data is likely to improve the decisions that a manager takes, and have a direct effect on business growth as the company becomes consumer focused. Growing the business becomes easier, as known customer needs become opportunities more easily satisfied, and success becomes more guaranteed.

CASE STUDY

International publishers of maps and guides

Our experience is that the only managers who can state that market research can be used effectively are those who have used it, and who clearly confirm that they have benefited from it. Take the example of publishers in the map, atlas, travel guide and globe sector, publishing their titles in the UK and United States. Many of the managers stated that before they had access to market research they would take their decisions based on assumptions which were always positive. They assumed all of the following:

- Their company was the market leader.
- Their company had a high profile as a publisher.
- The leading product in the range was known and used by all.
- The market size was roughly twice the company's own sales.
- The company had achieved total penetration in the market.
- They had a clear perception of the trade's attitude towards the company, its products and how they were marketed.
- Their sales force was highly thought of and the company's advertising and promotions were successful.

This sector has set up research groups of publishers to develop data in the market, by annually researching the attitude of the trade to publishers' support, and polling consumers to find out who was buying and using the products. The group in the UK was founded by HarperCollins, the Automobile Association publishing, Ordnance Survey, Michelin UK, Geocenter and Jarrold. The US group was founded by US Geological Survey, NOAA, the International Map Trade Association, Michelin US, MapLink and National Geographic/Trails Illustrated.

In both the United States and the United Kingdom the common research activity was the consumer survey, designed to:

- define consumer purchase in the market;
- discover to which shops consumers go to buy the products;

- discover how customers use the products;
- assess awareness and impact of the publishers' communications.

Members of the Research Group have realized that the research has become very effective, as it has helped to increase sales of the products. They have stated that:

- The companies increased sales as they implemented change, as a direct result of their greater understanding of the dynamics of the market and of their own strengths and weaknesses.
- The companies changed the design of some of their products, making them more consumer friendly.
- The companies changed their sales and distribution systems, to optimize the use of their sales forces.
- The companies set up retailer training courses, using the new understanding of the market to 'win the hearts and minds' of retailers.
- The companies changed their point of sales material and sales support procedures to better meet the needs of retailers.

HINTS ON TRACKING TRENDS AND CHANGING DECISIONS

- Develop your own 'movie' of the market in which you operate by agreeing what data is essential to track trends.
- Use benchmark data at management meetings to identify the extent to which company activities have changed. Tracking trends from benchmark information will help to influence the customer oriented decisions that can be taken.
- Recognize the need for measuring market performance, and without talking about confidential information, approach competitors to set up a market share monitor. They will find it beneficial if you approach them in the right way, informing them that they will be able to identify your share of the market and how it compares with their share.

- Integrate the research programme into your sales and marketing planning. This will ensure that you build in the necessary 'pre-campaign' and 'post campaign' evaluations, and provide you with continuous feedback.
- Plot the trends on colour graphics, as this will aid the interpretation of information, and therefore aid decision making in the long term.
- Disseminate the information as much as possible, as the more that can be learnt about market trends the more customer focused the industry, the supplier, the manufacturers and retailers can be.

8 Getting the most out of business relationships with research companies

INTRODUCTION

Many companies do not have research specialists as employees and have few resources for completing a professional research survey. Therefore, there are many who contact research companies for advice, guidance, research management and interpretation. But a manager who is not used to doing this, or has done it and has not been satisfied with the outcome of the project or business relationship, is in need of guidelines about the strengths and weaknesses of working with other companies. Their experience of the market and their understanding of their company's competitive positioning in the sector will help the focus on product and service opportunities for growing the business.

Worldwide there are some 2,500 officially registered research companies, identified as professional research organizations as opposed to management consultants. Each has experience in various markets, specialist resources and portfolios of clients in different industry sectors. Some specialize in personal interviewing, others in telephone interviewing, and others in data analysis, consultancy and computing. For those who are not familiar with any of these aspects of research, it is essential to get referral on the details of the companies and their services. The Market Research Society in the UK, the American Marketing Association in the US and ESOMAR in Europe all publish international directories of research companies by industrial sector of their experience.

COMMISSIONING RESEARCH COMPANIES

There are essentially three types of situation that managers might find themselves in when deciding on developing a business relationship with a research company.

No knowledge, experience or previous business relationships with a research company

In such a situation as this, it is advisable for a manufacturer or service provider to select at least three organizations to contact. These organizations should be identified by the suitability of their resources and experience. Each of these is then asked to submit formal proposals, and the most appropriate is selected to complete the project.

Knowledge of research but a need for external resources as little in-house skill

In this situation, evaluation of potential companies might be on an informal basis. Asking three organizations about what they do in your particular area of interest would ascertain the relevance of their experience and probably add to your understanding of what could be achieved. It is likely that at least two companies will be invited to submit formal proposals for competitive pricing and methodology.

Dedicated to research and in need of developing the research programme, particularly for continuous surveys, tracking surveys and customer monitoring, with or without professional research skills

It is likely that this manager will have worked with a number of research companies and will know exactly which one he or she wants to work with for a long-term programme. He or she might approach another company to check the research pricing, but is more likely to select the first company for the knowledge of each other's activities and needs, modus operandi and involvement in the presenting and reporting process. After a period of time, long-term business relationships are developed and the joint relationship helps to enhance the research planning, analysis and the interpretation of the results.

If your organization is interested in contacting a research organization, it is also important to know that the Code of Conduct of the Market Research Society specifies elements of 'good practice' that suppliers need to take into account when responding to your request. It is also considered acceptable practice for research agencies to charge for their time for preparing a proposal, if they are one of more than three suppliers asked to submit one.

QUALIFICATIONS OF SUPPLIERS

Market research is a specialized management tool, as specialized as public relations, advertising development, campaign planning and computer systems development. Any company offering market research needs to prove some factors to ensure it is able to provide the support and guidance that is required. You need to know whether:

- there is good knowledge among the personnel in the company of your market, product or service;
- it has experience of researching the type of projects that relate to your research requirement, or marketing or sales problem;

- the company has the resources and skills necessary to complete the work you require;
- the company considers you and your problems, rather than fitting your situation to fill the resources of its standard services;
- the organization is a member of a professional association or institute, and what quality control procedures and reassurances this provides for the collection of the data and its reporting for professional independent research analysis.

Some managers use their advertising agencies for advice and for implementing some research activities. The five points above apply to their experience in completing research which is likely to be oriented towards developing creative communications only, and do not ensure that they provide the breadth of experience that may be required for evaluating sales and marketing problems. In these later situations it is more effective to appoint a research consultancy or agency to complete research rather than an advertising agency.

Many research organizations find it difficult to communicate or sell their experience, and are unlike consultancies in this regard. They confuse protecting the confidentiality of the clients they have worked for and the projects they have worked on, which they have to honour under research industry codes of conduct, with describing their knowledge and providing good advice. Managers evaluating companies need to look for those companies whose written materials and verbal communications add to their understanding and knowledge of the subject being researched. Comments such as 'Have you thought of...' 'When we last researched this area we found...' 'The implications of what you are interested in doing are...' 'I would advise the project is carried out by...' all indicate a specific experience and knowledge to draw on and work with. Their skills are likely to complement your own knowledge and skills of sales marketing in your sector, and therefore these are appropriate organizations to select.

Other important factors for evaluating the service of a supplier to assist in your research project are its interest, experience and capability for making recommendations and listing actionable issues that may need further discussion within your own company.

The supplier needs to be able to talk about how the results of research have been used by other clients it has worked with, but without giving away confidential information. Many research agencies are just 'information houses' and do not see it as their role to provide advice and guidance. However, the competitiveness of the research industry is such that more and more suppliers are realizing that they need to help the information user to use the data. Those interested in doing this also have to be evaluated for their experience in providing this service, and for the value it is claimed to have added.

There is a difference between a research company that uses the summary of the key findings as its list of recommendations, and the company that adds to the summary at least six points which relate to sales, marketing or communications actions which management can discuss and act on. It is important to be aware and to be sure that independent advice on interpretation of data relates to the initial objectives of the project and answers any problems that were highlighted as topics or issues to be evaluated.

STANDARDS

Three sets of standards are worth seeking out in suppliers of market research – ethics, competence, and process - as an assurance of both reliability and quality.

Ethics

There are many references in this book to the Market Research Society Code of Conduct, which is based on the Code of the International Chambers of Commerce (ICC) and ESOMAR. The Code is the ethical framework within which genuine market research should be undertaken. The fundamental principles are:

> Research is founded upon the willing cooperation of the public and business organizations. It depends upon their confidence that it is conducted honestly, objectively, without unwelcome intrusion, and without harm to respondents. Its purpose is to collect and analyse information, and not directly to create sales, nor to influence the opinions of anyone participating in it. It is in this spirit that the Code of Conduct has been devised.
>
> The general public and other interested parties shall be entitled to complete assurance that every research project is carried out strictly in accordance with this Code, and that their rights of privacy are respected.

In particular, they must be assured that no information that could be used to identify them will be made available without their agreement to anyone outside the agency responsible for conducting the research. They must also be assured that the information they supply will not be used for any purposes other than research and that they will not be adversely affected or embarrassed as a direct result of their participation in a research project.

Wherever possible, respondents must be informed as to the purpose of the research and the likely length of time necessary for the collection of the information. Finally, the research findings themselves must always be reported accurately and never used to mislead anyone, in any way.

Competence

The level of knowledge and competence attained by individual researchers can normally be ascertained by verifying whether they have full professional status within their professional association. This is generally achieved via a degree-level education plus vocational training leading to a qualification, along with a minimum period of experience.

Professional status varies in different countries. The qualifications with the widest recognition are those offered internationally by the Market Research Society – the Advanced Certificate and Diploma in Market and Social Research Practice, details of which can be obtained by visiting the Market Research Society Web site (see www.mrs.org.uk/qualifications).

Standards

In the United Kingdom, the Market Research Quality Standards Association has formulated a set of process and service standards, which have been adopted by the British Standards Institution as BS7911. Market research is the first service sector to attain a British Standard, which is normally applied to physical materials and manufacturing processes.

Those who attain the standard are subject to independent audit inspection visits to ensure that the requirements continue to be met. The standard defines minimum requirements across all major parts of the research process – managing the executive element of research, data collection and data processing.

Comparable standards are now being adopted in many European countries, and plans are being made to seek accreditation by the International Standards Organization (ISO). Such process standards will become increasingly important in international research projects, particularly for organizations that commission research studies via their purchasing departments.

A SHORT BRIEF IS NOT A GOOD BRIEF

An important part of developing and establishing a good business relationship is for you, as a manager, to communicate clearly why you require an external company to provide you with support, and to describe what support you believe you need. The experienced researcher knows that a short brief is a bad brief, as it is unlikely to describe what is required. It is also likely to reflect poor knowledge of doing research and confusion on the part of the commissioning company, as the brief is unlikely to have been discussed internally as part of a discussion about what could be achieved by the research. An ill thought out brief can also lead to developing a research project which is inadequately structured, and thus results in information that is not relevant or conclusions that are unrealistic to the market conditions, structure of the company or planned marketing activity. Therefore it is important to develop a good brief.

Example of a brief brief

An example of a 'brief' brief is given on page 170. It is not specific enough, as it does not:

- provide background information on the company and the trends in the market;
- provide a definition of the objectives of the project;
- specify what are the purposes of each of the parts of the project;
- specify clearly all elements of the target market to be researched;
- specify in which countries the research should be completed;
- indicate the research hypothesis, information needs or objectives of using the data;

■ indicate the expected 'deliverables' that are essential for developing an effective business relationship.

Developing a good brief also ensures that the research involves all managers in the project and gives them the opportunity of thinking through why they need data, and how they are going to use it. This helps to get the project results accepted by the management in a company.

I have attended many presentations of research projects to a large management group when a member of the team has queried the research or phraseology of a question. Usually they are people who have not been consulted about the project and who have not had a chance to think about the information and the interpretations and absorption of the facts being presented. I have also seen situations where someone has become quite objectionable about the findings of the research analysis and has very noisily disrupted the meeting. Usually these are managers who have been invited into the meeting five minutes before it started, and they have not been briefed on the meeting, the purpose of the research or what information has been collected. So this can be a problem.

CLARITY AND DETAIL GET GOOD RESULTS

Some managers take the view that a research agency should be able to provide them with all the support they need without being given much in the way of background company or market information, as they are thought to be 'experts' on the market. This is a naive view, as the research company cannot envisage the internal political situations of a commissioning company, marketing plans that are being discussed or ideas that need to be tested out. It is essential to share these issues with a research company, as they have an effect on the project design, questionnaire construction and interpretation of the results.

Other managers say that they do not participate in market research because when they have done so in the past they have not learnt from it, and anything that has emerged from the research they already knew. It is these managers who have not thought about the research and have not prepared a clear and detailed brief. It is important to decide in what way the research should provide new information.

EXAMPLE OF A GOOD BRIEF

An example of a good brief is given on page 171. The key constituents of a good brief are:

- An introduction, giving background company and market information and the reasons for the project.
- A review of the sales, marketing or communications issues, the research hypothesis and how it relates to this situation.
- Details of the target market to be researched, and whether the company will provide the sample or specifications for the research company to work on when completing the sample for the interview.
- Comments on any previous research data or statistics that might help in planning the research project. This includes the market universe, penetration of products in the market, awareness of the company and so on.
- Any specific information requirements and areas that need detailed probing or analysis.
- The schedule needed for the publication of results.
- The budget and financial specifications for the business relationship.
- Any data or company information that is required to illustrate the brief and what is contained in it.

This approach to developing the business relationship with the researchers is advantageous to any manager using it. If comparisons between research companies are made in deciding who to commission, this identifies the parameters and a judgement on the best company to use can be taken comparatively. If a busy manager already knows which research company to use, the document is a detailed briefing which lays out the way in which the research management is to be completed, and all members of the team are clear as to what can be achieved. It becomes the project management plan.

The final commitment to the business relationship has to come from the research company proposing to do the project. It must lay out how it will organize the project and how it will deliver the requirements to the commissioning company. But even these documents should not be totally definitive: it is important for the research company to recognize that during the project there will be opportunity for development of the ideas and methodology and revision to the proposed business relationship.

QUALITY PROPOSAL DOCUMENTS FROM SUPPLIERS

Just as there are good and bad briefs, equally there are good and bad proposals from researchers. A comparative analysis of the way in which proposal documents are written shows whether the company has the right experience to do the research.

Example of a bad proposal

A bad proposal, like the sample one on page 173, is one that is not 'tailor made' to the commissioning company's needs as identified in the brief. It is likely to be too brief, not provide sufficient information of what happens in the project, when it happens and whether there is a perception of where problems might emerge. It might give details of a specific research service the research company runs, but it might not relate to the commissioning company why this service is appropriate for the project required. It might contain too many of the following phrases, which essentially indicate that the brief has not been thought through and that the company does not have the right experience to do the work. 'Until we have discussed...', 'It is not clear...', We cannot comment on...'. This is not fantasy, but an account of what can be seen in reality. Such a situation directly affects the quality of the project that is carried out, and the conclusions that are made when the research in finished.

Example of a good proposal

A good proposal is one that has the following characteristics, as in the sample on page 175. It has an introduction which not only acknowledges the content of the brief that has been provided, but also details additional information on the market, product and communications. This helps to show the commissioning company that the research company knows the market. Some research agencies call this section a 'discussion' but I always find it difficult to see how one can have a discussion with a written document. There is seldom any dialogue in it, which might indicate that it is a discussion!

The proposal should state the rationale and the objectives of the project. Specific objectives can be listed in addition to this, to indicate what can be achieved, particularly illustrating aspects of the service the company wants to provide – for example, 'to provide sales, marketing and communications recommendations'. It must also state and describe the research methodology, why it has been selected, the implications of using it, and issues that determine the success of using it. This section should also contain:

- any advice gained from the experience of the research company doing similar projects;
- details of the sample and sampling method and any problems associated with this initial part of the project;
- perceived problems or areas for discussion with alternative solutions, to inform management and help them to decide what to do;
- an indication of the question areas to be covered and what issues need to be discussed about the questions that will be asked.

Details of the fees and expenses and the terms and conditions of doing business with the commissioning company must be included in the proposal. The agency should also state why it believes it is the right company to do the work, and provide details of its previous experience and client portfolio. Finally, the proposal should include any other data or supporting information that the company believes is relevant to the client or the project.

A well written proposal is likely to get managers nodding in agreement while reading it. It should also be a document that the manager can pass around to other colleagues, as it should be self-explanatory about the project and what it is intending to achieve.

CONCLUSION

Unless your company employs in-house marketing research specialists who can run all elements of a market research project with your own company's resources, it will be necessary to use independent research suppliers. These organizations need to be selected for their experience, and become additional to the sales and marketing planning activities – their personnel have to perform like research managers, even though they are employed to support your company on a project basis.

When an effective business relationship is developed it can be beneficial to work with one or a selection of companies on a longer-term basis, and even pay a retainer fee for exclusive commitment to your company and your sales and marketing plan.

Achieving a constructive business relationship depends on being clear and cooperative in the conduct of the relationship. The mechanics of the project and the resources and facilities of the research agency are less important than its understanding of the market and its ability to interpret the sales and marketing implications of the research results. Good working relationships with research suppliers will help to ensure that good quality research results are provided. If the business relationship between your company and the research supplier is developed, the research supplier is likely to find it motivating to help your business to grow.

HINTS ON GETTING THE MOST OUT OF BUSINESS RELATIONSHIPS WITH RESEARCH COMPANIES

- Contact a specialist in your own industry to get a quality service complementing your own experience and market knowledge. If you are not certain who concentrates on your sector, visit the Web sites of the Market Research Society or the American Marketing Association and get a list of companies who claim sector experience.
- Check carefully the research experience of the company you want to work. Do not select the company because it claims to have completed a lot of work in your sector unless you feel the experience of the company adds to the work and project tasks that your team is working on.
- A research supplier who is not prepared to give advice and guidance on the results and implications of research may tend to give you statistics you already have. A company that is interested in giving

advice and recommendations will approach the project in an analytical way and therefore is more likely to improve the project design. The result of this will be agreement on information that will aid certain decisions, and the research company will be able to make its own interpretation of how the data affects these decisions.

▪ Write a clear brief, as you would expect to be briefed. Do not make it a 'brief' brief. Think carefully about who is going to be using the data. Ensure that they are involved in the project planning and implementation. This will help to avoid misunderstandings and bad briefing.

▪ Evaluate research company proposals carefully. A good proposal is one which includes comments such as 'In our experience ...' and 'Our knowledge of researching this sector encourages us to advise ...'.

▪ Write letters confirming all conversations in planning and implementing projects. Research suppliers are busy organizations and unless your requirements are detailed on paper there is a danger that a point discussed in a telephone conversation could be forgotten until it is too late.

▪ Recognize that if your requirements change at any time during the project, it is likely to change the business relationship. New ideas and new issues to be evaluated may not be included in the project easily. They may affect the costs and timing of the research, and imposing them on the original relationship may have an impact on the quality of the project.

▪ Try to develop a close working relationship with the supplier. If you tell the supplier everything about your requirements and brief its staff well you will get quality research, and relevant and actionable results. Research companies are not soothsayers and do not employ magicians. They are only going to produce a surprise out of the hat if you do exploratory customer research, which reveals information you do not already have.

A BRIEF BRIEF

Introduction

Brieffacts Ltd will be commissioning a large amount of work aimed at continuing the support of its products and services. The work will fall into the following areas:

- point of sales materials;
- training materials;
- advertising support;
- sales incentive campaigns;
- pricing strategies;
- distribution development;
- new product development.

In addition the company is interested in looking to develop its profile in the retail sector. Below are some of the identified issues that are relevant:

- branding of products for each target market;
- database management for communicating with existing and potential customers;
- market research, identifying perceived weaknesses and strengths and then actioning plans to respond to the findings.

I would therefore like to invite you to present your ideas on how you can add value to our decision making. An important part of the presentation will be information on your quality standards, and how they add to the quality of the project.

The proposals must be presented ten days from receipt of this brief.

A GOOD BRIEF

Introduction

Specific Facts Ltd is a major service organization with 150,000 customers. It is proposing to carry out a customer satisfaction survey among its trade, consumer and business and professional customers. The purpose of this survey is to evaluate customer satisfaction relating to the company and the products. This is particularly important as the company has decided to launch a series of new products in what is essentially a very competitive market. It therefore wants to ensure that its current customers remain loyal and committed to the company, its products and services.

This research survey is being offered to tender and you are invited to present an outline of how the survey would be approached, giving details of experience, methodology, timings and fees, and who will manage the project.

Methodology

The survey is to be carried out by telephone interviews as the number of questions is relatively small, and the questionnaire will contain both pre-coded and open-ended questions. The majority of it will involve 'attribute' ratings on products and services, based on some existing qualitative research.

Sample

Specific Facts Ltd has 50,000 trade, 50,000 consumer, 25,000 business and 25,000 professional customers, and all these are listed in a name and address computerized marketing information system. This list has been segmented by user type, geographic area and sales per year, to ensure that it is representative of the different types of customer. This list can be supplied to the agency within the terms of data protection legislation, and deployed in accordance with the Code of Conduct of the Market Research Society.

Topic areas for research

The key areas of information that will help the company to determine its customer service strategy are:

- contact with the company;
- evaluation of accessibility to the company;
- speed of problem solving;
- speed of responsiveness;
- quality of communications;
- assessment of products;
- attitudes to:
  - technical support;
  - price;
  - promotions;
  - delivery;
  - problem solving.

Reporting

We will need to have the results presented to the project team prior to submission of the final report.

The final report will need to include a summary and list of actions that are viewed important to consider as a result of the research.

Budget

The project cost is not expected to exceed £25,000.

Timing

The project will be commissioned in July 2004 and has to be completed for a customer conference presentation to all the company's customers in September 2004. It will be updated annually.

A BRIEF PROPOSAL

Introduction

Brief Proposal Ltd has been asked to provide a proposal for carrying out a customer satisfaction study on behalf of Brieffacts Ltd. The purpose of the survey is to evaluate the level of customer satisfaction with the products and services provided by Brieffacts Ltd.

The brief

Brieffacts Ltd produces a range of products that are sold into two main market sectors:

- agents and trade outlets;
- professional and business end-users.

It is estimated from its customer base of 150,000 that a high proportion are regular customers. Of these 80 per cent fall into the second category, and it is this segment that is to be included in the sample for the customer satisfaction survey.

Brief Proposal Ltd will be supplied with the sample to be telephoned in either disc or label format. It is likely that telephone numbers will be supplied in most cases. If not they will be number searched. The sample itself will be made up of a selection of professional and business customers, including local and state government, utilities, government agencies, real estate firms and lawyers. The data to be gathered will cover the following areas:

- services used;
- level of service provided by Brieffacts Ltd staff;
- clarity of invoicing and delivery documentation;
- quality of product;
- which agent was used most recently;
- quality of service provided by agent;
- quality of product provided by agent.

The majority of the questions will be closed, although it is anticipated that at least one open question will be included.

All information gathered during the call will then be entered on to disc and analysed.

Methodology

Information gathered during the project will initially be recorded manually on a questionnaire. All questionnaires will then be sight verified and input to disc. The benefits of having a two-stage approach, as opposed to inputting directly to computer, are:

- It allows 100 per cent concentration on the interview.
- It creates a more personable and natural interview.
- Data is verified twice, once before inputting and once after.
- Specialists are used for both stages of the process.

All data input to disc is again sight verified before any analysis is carried out.

Reporting and analysis

A daily report will be produced which will encompass the following areas:

- number of calls made;
- number of completed questionnaires;
- number of refusals;
- call rate.

At the end of the research, a detailed report will be produced which will consist of counts of all the questions together with any cross-tabulations that are required. Detailed written analysis will be given on a question-by-question basis, and a general summary will cover all the main conclusions of the campaign.

Brief Proposal Ltd currently employs 25 full-time salaried staff. In addition to this, we have over 60 trained temporary staff who are used on a project-by-project basis.

Cost breakdown

Set up, calling charges, data entry, reporting and analysis and management fee: Total £20,750.

All costs are quoted exclusive of VAT and subject to the terms and conditions of Brief Proposal Ltd. Payment terms to be agreed.

A DETAILED PROPOSAL

Introduction

Detailed Proposal Ltd plans a customer monitor survey among its business and professional customers. Details of 150,000 customers are held on a database, which will be used for the research. This document seeks to explain how we would approach a study of this nature, and takes certain assumptions about sample design and timing. Such matters are clearly open for discussion should we be awarded the project.

The sample

The customer database should be the main source of the sample. However, customer monitor surveys can sometimes be accused of working within a vacuum. This is because people generally become customers of an organization if at one time (if not currently) they are satisfied that what they will be receiving (in terms of product or service) will generally be in line with their expectations. Having taken the decision to buy at some point, they will have been *de facto* more satisfied than those who could have purchased, but did not.

The people who are ignored by this process are therefore lapsed customers, competitor customers or non-customers of some other kind. Research among existing customers can therefore only address their needs. Lapsed and/or competitor customers may have entirely different views and needs.

While it is true that customer satisfaction research is, by definition, a measurement of (current) users or buyers, its purpose is generally to retain or increase the customer base. In the latter case, it is our view that lapsed or non-customers should always be addressed.

The reason that lapsed or non-customers are neglected is frequently practicality. Rarely is lapsing an action that is recorded. Organizations that have never been customers, but could be, are difficult to find systematically.

There are two different types of sample. The first is a quota of particular groups to ensure the sample is representative. In other words, if 20 per cent of the customer database comprises state authorities, then 20 per cent of the sample should also. Provided the sample is selected randomly, it should naturally fall out this way. However, careful sample management is necessary to ensure that this is the case, since the required number of interviews can quickly be achieved by calling easier to reach respondents, rather than those who are harder to make contact with and perhaps need several call-back attempts. Typically, personnel in larger organizations and more senior personnel tend to be harder to reach. A simple quota can avoid this potential source of bias.

The second type of quota is set in order to yield sufficient numbers of interviews with particular groups or concerns. Thus, if 5 per cent of the customer base is lawyers in private practices and the total sample for the study is 500, only 25 lawyers will be interviewed. Such a sample is too small to provide meaningful comparative results. It is common therefore to set a quota of a minimum number of interviews.

In order to yield results that are representative of the total customer base, two sets of data need to be produced. The first is a 'weighted set', which re-sorts the subsample sizes to their true incidence across the database. The second is 'unweighted', to look at each of the subsamples individually.

The third type of quota is one that is based on information derived only from the interview, not from the database. If for example Detailed Proposal Ltd wish to speak to a number of people who have contacted the company by fax, and this information is not available on the database, a quota can be set for this. However accurate costing of such a quota is impossible until at least part of the fieldwork is complete, since the incidence will not be known until this point.

It is important that a sufficient contact sample exists for each quota cell, and that the quota matrix is not elaborate, since this will have a major bearing on the project costs.

Sample preparation

We are assuming that the customer database is available as a computer record and we can access this information within the framework of the data protection legislation and the Code of Conduct of the Market Research Society. We are able to select a sample from a diskette of the database, should this be available. This avoids duplicated labour and means that other information (perhaps sales ordering history) can be loaded on to the sample datafile and used for subsequent cross-analysis.

The questionnaire

We have assumed that the interview length will average 15 minutes. Since the research is required to measure satisfaction across a number of dimensions, we would not recommend the use of open-ended questions since these tend to produce considerable rates of error (particularly for attitudinal-type questions). We have allowed for only two to three such questions in our costing.

We would suggest, regardless of our involvement in its design, that the questionnaire be piloted in real time prior to release to main fieldwork. This involves achieving six interviews and holding an informal debrief to establish whether any slight rewording is appropriate.

The research method

All interviews will be conducted by telephone from a central location.

The questionnaires will be administered using Computer Assisted Telephone Interviewing (CATI) equipment. This facility enables the questionnaire to flow automatically according to the answers given by each respondent, and handles rotations and text substitution routines automatically. CATI also prevents logic errors, which are inevitable when a questionnaire is administered on paper.

The sample will be controlled using a Telephone Number Management System (TNMS). This handles callback routines, appointments, reasons for non-response and so on, and is of great value in maximizing response rates. Up to four attempts will be made to secure an interview.

All interviewers are given a thorough training, regardless of claimed experience in other companies. All are specifically trained in business-to-business interviewing. Call monitoring is also used to monitor interviewer quality.

Other fieldwork quality control standards will exceed the minimum laid down by the Interviewer Quality Control Scheme (IQCS), of which we are a member. Membership of the scheme is dependent upon a successful annual inspection.

Reporting

In customer monitor research, it is important to establish not just how individual services or departments perform, but how important each of these is in affecting satisfaction overall. In this way, an organization can set priorities for action by concentrating on those areas that will impact satisfaction most. Multiple regression is the best method available to determine this, and we have considerable expertise in this area. However, this form of analysis can be quite time consuming and we have therefore included it only as an option.

If it is planned to repeat the study at some point in the future, a regression approach would be particularly useful. This is because customer expectations are a moving target. What is less important in one year may appear more so the next. This method will ensure that such a trend can be identified.

This analysis may also be used to generate a scoring system against which to set goals and measure relative performance. The process works by asking respondents to rate the performance (delivery) of a particular aspect of the service. Different points are allocated to each, based upon its importance, as measured by the regression, and its delivery based on the performance rating. In this way, more points can be gained or lost depending upon how well each aspect is delivered. Such a process of data reduction can simplify the results, making them more easily assimilated, thus improving the value of the study across the organization.

We will provide two copies of the data tables. In addition, up to 50 summary charts will be produced to our specification in graphical format as a PowerPoint file.

Schedule

The following schedule appears realistic:

Study commission	25 May 2004
Agreement of first draft of questionnaire	27 May 2004
Final draft	30 May 2004
Questionnaire pilot	5 June 2004
Sampling and CATI set-up	8 June 2004
Fieldwork commences	10 June 2004
Fieldwork ends	26 June 2004
Coding & data preparation	30 June 2004
Data tables	3 July 2004
Charts & regression analysis	7 July 2004

Our fees are subject to agreement of final questionnaire, sample structure and our terms of business. These call for settlement of 50 per cent of the survey value to be payable within 30 days of commission and the balance within 30 days of receipt of final tables and charts.

For 500 interviews including:

- questionnaire design assistance;
- CATI set-up;
- sampling;
- fieldwork;
- coding and data preparation;
- analysis (1 table per question);
- PowerPoint charts,

the cost will be £24,950.00 plus VAT @ 17.5 per cent.

Regression analysis

This option will incur an additional fee of £3,500 plus VAT.

Our experience

Detailed Proposal Ltd provides a range of qualitative and quantitative research services to business and government agencies. The company concentrates on building a long-term relationship with its clients, believing that our contribution increases the more we understand a client's business. Research is conducted within the US, Europe and increasingly Asia Pacific.

The company has established a reputation for premium quality telephone research. At the core of the company is a 55-station telephone centre equipped with CATI and full remote listening and VDU monitoring facilities. Other areas of particular expertise are in technology products and financial services. We have conducted many studies with professional groups including real estate, lawyers, architects and construction companies.

9 Using research to grow your business

INTRODUCTION

As research becomes more strategic in its contribution to companies, the role of the researcher will become more important. The independent analyst can make an effective, positive and additional contribution to decision making using market knowledge, analytical experience and a clearer understanding of competitive market forces. The researcher will therefore become more effective than a communications strategist or planner. He or she will fulfil the role of corporate planner for the smaller company, and strategic market analyst in the larger company. But the contribution the researcher will make will be more fundamental in creating a market-led strategy than a communications planner, as it will relate much more to the needs of the market than to creative themes designed to attract the market's attention irrespective of their needs.

Companies will want to ensure that they perform profitably in more competitive markets. Market assumptions will become less reliable than using hard market data to understand, evaluate and monitor the implementation of the sales and marketing methods required.

Every manager needs to review the role for research within the company and gain management agreement and commitment on how it can be used effectively. The most effective roles, which can help companies devise the best methods to expand business, are to make the research and information function central to the decision making process and to use better data in all management meetings than is descriptive of just the sales analysis.

It is important to develop systems that are central to the whole running of the company and that input and output both internal and external data. This data needs to be used to devise which sales, marketing and communications methods are required, which are effective and which need to have more resources allocated to help increase sales.

Managers cannot take the wrong decisions if they set up systems that regularly provide key facts which help them to identify whether the sales and marketing process is progressing successfully. Brand share data will provide the statistics on how well sales are being achieved competitively. If collected in a detailed analysis this can help to establish which product categories should be developed or stimulated through promotional support to counter competitive threat.

Developing customer data and defining the user and buyer characteristics, buying habits and the nature of the customer needs within the total market will provide the key information on how to anticipate, respond to and sell to defined customer needs. An important part of this is to establish, understand and interpret the language of your customers, as it will help to confirm your company's competitive unique selling points. Once these have been defined, all sales, marketing and communications methods can reflect these unique selling points and emphasize the benefits of your products and services competitively.

Once the target market is defined and the customer trends are realized, it is important to segment the customers into categories that make the sales and marketing effort cost effective in its delivery. This is essential for growing the business, as each market segment requires a different approach for all sales and marketing techniques. These segments also relate to how new products and services can be developed for the subgroups that exist within the customer base. It is important for a manager to analyse the segments clearly and understand how the trends and needs differ within each segment. Computer techniques to define the factors and clusters that exist, relating the segments to life style and classification characteristics, will improve the market analysis and provide the manager with targets that respond more specifically to customer-focused sales and marketing methods. Creating your own 'map' of your market and how the segments map in conjunction with the segments' trends and lifestyles, provides the best way of measuring your sales and marketing methods in the market.

Data that has been collected and analysed well also needs to be presented and reported with relevance. The data needs to address the sales and marketing problems, competitive positioning and the company's internal political issues, which must be considered useful information. It is also important that whatever data is collected generates clear recommendations, ideas or issues that contribute to management thinking, idea generation and strategic planning. This ensures that the information that is collected is used, and its use makes a significant contribution to business planning.

When developing research programmes it is important to create a positive and constructive business relationship with the research supplier. Use of the research supplier to prove or disprove an internal political issue, such as getting work done more efficiently externally than internal resources can provide, is not a sensible or profitable use of management time. Equally if the research supplier is expected to perform without laying out the parameters in which it can support your company, it is not a good investment in using market specialists.

Provide the research supplier with clear and well thought out information, and it will be effective in responding to you in the same way

CASE STUDY

Publishers: using research to grow their business

Companies that have benefited from using research to grow their businesses are those that have planned the research effectively. For example, publishers that have used research to take their decisions have said that a number of benefits have been realized (although they have only been doing this research for 18 years, which is a limited timespan in trend analysis):

- understanding their share of the market, and knowing their penetration in the different segments of the market;
- identifying where their sales have been effective and where further support is required to increase sales;
- better targeting to current and potential customers to communicate product and service benefits;
- more realistic budgeting, which has related to estimating sales and allocating the right amount of resources to increase sales;
- understanding the customers of their customers – both retailers and end users – and giving retailers better information on the needs of customers visiting stores.

Research for these companies has become an effective planning, monitoring and ongoing decision making tool, central to the whole process of customer-led decision making.

RESEARCH FOR THE FUTURE

The company of the new century will be one that has a good marketing information system providing a comparison between internal and external information. The management of the company will want to use information to monitor customer care and how well customers are satisfied. Data will become more significant, as it will be used to prove to customers how satisfied other customers are with the style and delivery of customer service. The managers will also want to see their market shares, to check competitive sales activity and have sufficient information to know whether success is continuing or changing.

A user and attitude survey and an awareness and attitude survey will help to develop trend data if run by a company regularly. This trend data will monitor customers' attitudes to products and promotions planning. Reviewing it will influence the decisions that are taken as a result, by improving customer targeting or developing better promotional copy, or redesigning products or services to correspond to changing consumer demand.

Research provides the means of getting a clear understanding of the market and the focus of market needs. It provides the mechanism for feedback and monitoring management decisions and their effectiveness.

As the role of the sales force changes, so the crucial importance of research in focusing and prioritizing sales actions increases. Since the early 1990s the sales task increasingly has been tested to prove to chosen customers that a company's products or services will meet their commercial requirement better than competitors'. Thus the sales function must be concerned with helping to achieve customers' key objectives, be they profit, growth or market share. Nowadays the sales force is concerned with understanding customers' financial pressures, industry, processes, customers and markets, and their internal procedures and policies. As a consequence, the salesperson must have not only up-to-date quantitative information on all these customer aspects, but most importantly there must be qualitative assessment of how the customer views, judges and values the sales proposition compared with all the competitive offerings. Without regular up-to-date research on all these aspects, the sales force will be at a severe disadvantage to their competitors and customers. Denied these vital pieces of information, the salesperson is like a fully equipped infantryman without ammunition. No bullets – no bull's-eyes!

Research defines who to sell your product to, in a way that the target customers relate to, through their understanding of how the product or service meets their needs, provided it is marketed in a consumer-friendly manner. Using research to grow your business depends on more proactive managers recognizing that their company needs a culture of using information in this way. Where research becomes effective in increasing sales is in guiding managers to change their preconceptions and previous decisions, and updating them in line with changing consumer needs.

Growing the business may present its complexities and uncertainties. Using market research to grow the business does not just reduce the risk, it helps management to confirm that their decisions have a competitive edge and will result in achieving new sales, and eventually committed customers. Market research is only effective if it is actioned, considered and assessed, and used to produce tangible benefits to the running and development of the business.

Companies also know that as a result of these changes, they have increased their penetration of the market, increased their market share, increased consumer and retailer awareness, and as a result, increased sales. They therefore have realized that the effective use of market research is communications actions.

There are times when a company has no grasp of a new market or the operating mechanisms within it. Desk research will outline the size or the 'ball park' and maybe some of the segmentation, but only a consumer user and attitude survey can give the whys and wherefores, the current product pluses and minuses. You can look upon this information rather like a nail in the wall. Where you have a nail, you can hang a picture. It may not be in the right place but you can adjust that later. However, no nail – no picture!

CASE STUDIES ON HOW TO GROW YOUR BUSINESS

Let us then examine two results from the meat industry, again from the sausage casings firm referred to earlier. The casing, while only a small part of the sausage in term of weight, has a highly important role to play. The casing is the primary point of product contact with the consumer, and conveys a plethora of images and ideas about the total product. Is the sausage it contains succulent, appetising, meaty – in fact, a quality item the consumer should buy? Get the casing and the imagery correct, and the sausages zip their way from shelf to checkout, but get it wrong and the poor sausage languishes its shelf life away. By simply changing casings it is possible to give a sausage an entirely different consumer profile.

The first example concerns a product change introduced by a large US multinational that ought to have done its homework better. It is also a very good example of why the classic sales statement 'This is a large and experienced customer. He knows what he is doing' should normally be ignored. Size is no indication of quality.

The large multinational decided to change the type and also the supplier of the casing on one of its core sausage products. The advantage of this move to the multinational was a 5 per cent drop in the purchase price of the casing (less than 0.5 per cent of the overall product cost). No big deal, you may say: the original supplier just matches the new, competitive casing price and retains the business. However it was not as simple as that. The product to be bought instead had a significantly cheaper raw material source than the original product. Thus the argument of price match was invalid, as the new supplier with the cheaper raw material source would have won any game of price reduction.

What was to be done, as there was no traditional sales argument that would retain the business for the supplier? The performance of both products in the sausage factories was the same, and price favoured the newcomer. The multinational made the change and gleefully accepted the price benefits.

The old supplier, not wishing to lose the business, decided to test both products with consumers and arranged for a paired comparison to be done. The results were entirely in its favour, with consumers giving a 60 per cent overall preference to the sausage in its casing and only 40 per cent going for the new competitor. That in itself should have been enough to convince the multinational to rescind the decision, for to persist would have meant a drop in product sales.

Closer examination of the research results showed even more. Regular consumers of the sausages, who stated a continuing interest in future purchase, had a strong preference for the qualities imparted by the original casing, while the new, cheaper alternative appealed only to those who were irregular purchasers of the sausages, with a low interest in future purchase. In essence, consumers were saying through the research that the change would be terminally bad for future sale of sausages with the new cheaper casing. Results like this in the food market tend to indicate the demise of the offending product within a year.

The original supplier presented the results to the multinational, which took heed, but due to various internal machinations it took five months to reverse its decision. At the end of that period sales for the sausage in the new casing were only 33 per cent of what they had been five months previously!

So you see the research has a role. Consumers did not like the change and voted with their feet. The multinational was in danger of losing its complete sausage product business for the sake of a 5 per cent cost saving on one component, or less than 0.5 per cent of the overall finished product cost. The moral of this story: research everything that alters the product, or even might alter it, in terms of consumer perception.

After the change back to the original specification, product sales rose to their pre-change levels within four months. Research proved to be accurate and useful to both the consumer and the supplier. Both companies continued to earn money from their respective products, a state which would not have existed had the research not been done and the mistake been allowed to eliminate the product.

The second example is in the same sector and concerns the potential destruction of a market. The Polish sausage market is one of the largest in Europe. Following the tearing down of the Berlin Wall the market opened up to many casing products, particularly those from the west. This stimulated local competition, and a number of small producers emerged. Their products were cheap, but the quality was not always to acceptable standards. Sausages encased in these products wrinkled rapidly, as the casings had high water permeability, allowing water loss under chill. The resulting sausage looked wrinkled, aged and terrible.

Sausage producers, on the other hand, were primarily interested in price and were quite insistent that the wrinkling was not a consumer problem. Low product price, achieved by low component prices, was more important to the consumer, they confidently stated. One western sausage casing manufacturer was unconvinced. In fact, it was sure that the appearance of the sausages in store was rapidly downgrading the product's position and effectively destroying the market. So it set about proving the hypothesis. Market research was commissioned. A paired comparison was run, comparing sausages in a western casing and a locally produced Polish casing. All the parameters were identical, only the casing was different.

The results were dramatic. The sausage encased in the western casing was smooth, shiny and sleek after two weeks' storage, while its locally encased companion exhibited severe wrinkling. But the wrinkling does not matter, according to the sausage producers; it is price that is paramount. So price was tested too.

The outcome was as you might expect. The consumer preference for the western-encased product was 99 per cent. The consumers hated the wrinkles, and when asked about pricing, stated a willingness to purchase the preferred product at a substantial premium, as this product was seen to be better value for money. The research results were presented to the Polish sausage manufacturers, and were accepted. Furthermore, the data were so convincing that one of the manufacturers changed immediately to the western casing. The initial order paid for the research.

Market research in this case was not only effective in gaining business for the company that conducted it, but it was also effective in stopping the erosion of a market. There was a further benefit to the local sausage producers, in that they were able to use the research results to better position their products and to price them more efficiently. The outcome of the project thus had benefits for everybody – the supplier, the producer and last but not least, the consumer.

THE ACTION AFTER THE RESEARCH

On completion of the research, the information provided should be used to help management understand:

- the market in which the company is operating, and the implications of such an environment;
- the attitudes and motivations of the company's present and potential customers, and their criteria for selecting a company and its products or services in preference to competition;
- when new products and services are required, and how to design them to meet the changing needs of existing and new customers;
- how to use the selection criteria and attitudes of the customers to develop communications and promotional themes so that their needs are satisfied; the end result of this is to persuade them to buy the company's products rather than those of competitors.

CONCLUSION: USING RESEARCH IS A 'WIN-WIN' SITUATION

It is seldom that the completion of a market research programme does not provide the basis for action. All market research can be cost effective if it is designed to address the marketing and sales issues concerned. In order to do this, the company must:

- define carefully its marketing and communications strategy;
- agree the hypotheses or ideas that need to be proved or disproved to allow for the development of its strategy;
- research the total market and the mechanisms of that market, rather than just the product or communications issues related to the market;
- decide on the likely actions it could take after the research, to assess them through the research adopted or identify what other actions are more important;
- be prepared to use the findings of the research to improve the ways in which the company's total sales and marketing activities are run, and how they relate to customer buying behaviour.

Research is necessary to ensure the effectiveness of marketing, and thus it is not only a service to the marketing function: it is a means of directing the company to a successful future. A company has to:

- Accept that research is only of use if it is acted on; it is both ineffective and costly if used for information purposes only.
- Accept that research can provide a combination of information about the market, the strengths and weaknesses of its marketing methods, and how they relate to the needs of its customers.
- Monitor the size, shape and nature of its markets; the needs of its markets; the opportunities and threats within the market; the marketing required to meet them; the market gaps that exist, and which of them present key areas of interest for the marketing strategies of the future to be focused on and pursued.
- Collect information on competitors and know whether its strategic approach and chosen sales, marketing and communications strategies are better or worse than those of other suppliers in the sector.

It is important to know the 'state of health' of the market, and the performance of the company in the market, to the extent of measuring the success of individual sales and marketing methods. Without this knowledge a company cannot be sure of success and of taking the right decisions.

The action after the research is to use the research not only to take the right decisions, but also to decide on actions that are realistic in relation to the product or service being marketed and the consumer purchasing or using them. Research provides a company with the key to success when it is not merely solving a marketing problem, but has been carefully designed to provide direction and guidance for taking the right sales and marketing decisions.

Using research is a 'win-win' situation for those who interpret it and action it effectively. Management 'wins' first time when the research confirms its prejudices, ideas and experiences, so providing reassurances that it is taking the right decisions and indeed that the research was done correctly. It 'wins' a second time if the research provides new information or gives a new focus or emphasis on the subject being researched.

Over a period of time users of research also find that they 'win' a third time. If they take a step back to look at the original findings of the research objectively, they can design more interesting and more relevant research than had been completed originally. Research therefore helps management to 'win' by indicating the actions it needs to take.

CHECKLIST OF QUESTIONS FOR THE EFFECTIVE USE OF MARKET RESEARCH

- What decisions can I take?
- Which marketing consultancy company's experience will complement our requirements to help to take these decisions?
- Does the company have experience in our specific market?
- Do the company's executives understand not only the marketing problem, but also ultimately what decisions we are likely to be faced with?
- How valid are the research results?
- Are the desk research data derived from a reliable source?

■ Are the attitudes and opinions of the target sample sufficiently representative?

■ Does the questionnaire assess the market, as well as the needs of buyers and non-buyers, looking to prove or disprove the acceptance of new ideas or products in the marketplace?

■ Can the research brief only provide information, or will it also provide direction on our marketing and sales decisions?

■ What evaluation needs to be carried out to identify:
  - the effects of competitor's products and services?
  - the market segments that the company does not satisfy?
  - the behaviour of non-buyers or non-users?
  - the traditional, current and future uses of the products or services?
  - the benefits of the product or service?

■ What are the required actions after the research?

■ Do we know sufficiently well the market we are operating in and its products or services in preference to those of our competitors?

■ Do we know when new products and services are required, and how to design them to meet the changing needs of customers and potential customers?

■ How do we use the selection criteria and attitudes of customers to develop communication and promotional themes so that their motivations are satisfied?

■ How do we ensure that the company is taking all its decisions in the way that our customers think?

■ Will the research we have designed produce the desired actions after the research?

■ Have we agreed the hypotheses or ideas that need to be proved or disproved to allow for the development of the strategy?

■ Does the research cover the total market and the mechanisms of that market rather than just the product or communications issues related to that market?

■ Have we decided on the likely actions that we could take after the research, to assess them through the research adopted, or identify through the research what other actions are more important?

■ Are we prepared to use the findings of the research to improve the ways in which our total sales and marketing activities are run and how they relate to the way in which our customers buy the products or services?

- Are we prepared to act on the research?
- Are we sure that the research is not for information purposes only, and that it is both effective and cost effective?
- Can the research provide a combination of information about the market, the strengths and weaknesses of our marketing methods, and how they relate to the needs of our customers?
- Is it monitoring the size, shape and nature of our markets, the needs of our markets, the opportunities and threats within our market, the marketing required to meet them, the market opportunities, the market gaps that exist and which present key areas of interest for the marketing strategies of the future?
- Has the research been designed to provide a 'win-win' situation?
- Can we see 'life after the death of the research'?

Appendix: The Market Research Society Code of Conduct

INTRODUCTION

The Market Research Society

With over 8,000 members in more than 50 countries, The Market Research Society (MRS) is the world's largest international membership organisation for professional researchers and others engaged in (or interested in) marketing, social or opinion research.

It has a diverse membership of individual researchers within agencies, independent consultancies, client-side organisations, and the academic community, and from all levels of seniority and job functions.

All members agree to comply with the MRS Code of Conduct, which is supported by the Codeline advisory service and a range of specialist guidelines on best practice.

MRS offers various qualifications and membership grades, as well as training and professional development resources to support these. It is the official awarding body in the UK for vocational qualifications in market research.

MRS is a major supplier of publications and information services, conferences and seminars and many other meeting and networking opportunities for researchers.

MRS is 'the voice of the profession' in its media relations and public affairs activities on behalf of professional research practitioners, and aims to achieve the most favourable climate of opinions and legislative environment for research.

The purpose of the Code of Conduct

This edition of the Code of Conduct was agreed by The Market Research Society to be operative from July 1999. It is a fully revised version of a self-regulatory code which has been in existence since 1954. This Code is based upon and fully compatible with the ICC/ESOMAR International Code of Marketing and Social Research Practice. The Code of Conduct is designed to support all those engaged in marketing or social research in maintaining professional standards. It applies to all members of The Market Research Society, whether they are engaged in consumer, business to business, social, opinion or any other type of confidential survey research. It applies to all quantitative and qualitative methods for data gathering. Assurance that research is conducted in an ethical manner is needed to create confidence in, and to encourage co-operation among, the business community, the general public, regulators and others.

The Code of Conduct does not take precedence over national law. Members responsible for international research shall take its provisions as a minimum requirement and fulfil any other responsibilities set down in law or by nationally agreed standards.

The purpose of guidelines

MRS Guidelines exist or are being developed in many of these areas in order to provide a more comprehensive framework of interpretation. These guidelines have been written in recognition of the increasingly diverse activities of the Society's members, some of which are not covered in detail by the Code of Conduct. A full list of guidelines appears on the Society's Web site, and is also available from the Society's Standards Manager.

One particular guideline covers the use of databases containing personal details of respondents or potential respondents, both for purposes associated with confidential survey research and in cases where respondent details are passed to a third party for marketing or other purposes. This guideline has been formally accepted by the Society, following extensive consultation with members and with the Data Protection Registrar/Commissioner.

Relationship with data protection legislation

Adherence to the Code of Conduct and the database Guidelines will help to ensure that research is conducted in accordance with the principles of data protection legislation. In the UK this is encompassed by the Data Protection Act 1998.

Data protection definitions

Personal Data means data which relates to a living individual who can be identified

- from the data, or
- from the data and other information in the possession of, or likely to come into the possession of, the data controller

and includes any expression of opinion about the individual and any indication of the intentions of the data controller or any other person in respect of the individual.

Processing means obtaining, recording or holding the information or data or carrying out any operation or set of operations on the information or data, including

- organisation, adaptation or alteration
- retrieval, consultation or use
- disclosure by transmission, dissemination or otherwise making available
- alignment, combination, blocking, erasure or destruction.

It is a requirement of membership that researchers must ensure that their conduct follows the letter and spirit of the principles of Data Protection legislation from the Act. In the UK the eight data protection principles are.

- **The First Principle**
  Personal data shall be processed fairly and lawfully.[1]

- **The Second Principle**
  Personal data shall be obtained only for one or more specified and lawful purposes, and shall not be further processed in any manner incompatible with that purpose or those purposes.
- **The Third Principle**
  Personal data shall be adequate, relevant and not excessive in relation to the purpose or purposes for which they are processed.
- **The Fourth Principle**
  Personal data shall be accurate and, where necessary, kept up to date.
- **The Fifth Principle**
  Personal data processed for any purpose or purposes shall not be kept longer than is necessary for that purpose or those purposes.
- **The Sixth Principle**
  Personal data shall be processed in accordance with the rights of data subjects under this Act.
- **The Seventh Principle**
  Appropriate technical and organisational measures shall be taken against unauthorised or unlawful processing of personal data and against accidental loss or destruction of, or damage to, personal data.
- **The Eighth Principle**
  Personal data shall not be transferred to a country or territory outside the European Economic Area, unless that country or territory ensures an adequate level of protection for the rights and freedoms of data subjects in relation to the processing of personal data.

Exemption for research purposes

Where personal data processed for research, statistical or historical purposes are not processed to support decisions affecting particular individuals, or in such a way as likely to cause substantial damage or distress to any data subject, such processing will not breach the Second Principle and the data may be retained indefinitely despite the Fifth Principle.

As long as the results of the research are not published in a form, which identifies any data subject, there is no right of subject access to the data.

Code definitions

- **Research**
  Research is the collection and analysis of data from a sample of

individuals or organisations relating to their characteristics, behaviour, attitudes, opinions or possessions. It includes all forms of marketing and social research such as consumer and industrial surveys, psychological investigations, observational and panel studies.

■ **Respondent**

A respondent is any individual or organisation from whom any information is sought by the researcher for the purpose of a marketing or social research project. The term covers cases where information is to be obtained by verbal interviewing techniques, postal and other self-completion questionnaires, mechanical or electronic equipment, observation and any other method where the identity of the provider of the information may be recorded or otherwise traceable. This includes those approached for research purposes whether or not substantive information is obtained from them and includes those who decline to participate or withdraw at any stage from the research.

■ **Interview**

An interview is any form of contact intended to provide information from a respondent.

■ **Identity**

The identity of a respondent includes, as well as his/her name and/or address, any other information which offers a reasonable chance that he/she can be identified by any of the recipients of the information.

■ **Children**

For the Purpose of the Code, children and young people are defined as those aged under 18. The intention of the provisions regarding age is to protect potentially vulnerable members of society, whatever the source of their vulnerability, and to strengthen the principle of public trust. Consent of a parent or responsible adult should be obtained for interviews with children under 16. Consent must be obtained under the following circumstances:

- In home/at home (face-to-face and telephone interviewing)
- Group discussions/depth interviews
- Where interviewer and child are alone together.

Interviews being conducted in public places, such as in-street/in-store/central locations, with 14 and 15 years olds may take place without consent if a parent or responsible adult is not accompanying the child. In these situations an explanatory thank you note must be given to the child.

Under special circumstances, a survey may waive parental consent but only with the prior approval of the Professional Standards Committee.

- **Records**
  The term records includes anything containing information relating to a research project and covers all data collection and data processing documents, audio and visual recordings. Primary records are the most comprehensive record of information on which a project is based; they include not only the original data records themselves, but also anything needed to evaluate those records, such as quality control documents. Secondary records are any other records about the Respondent.
- **Client**
  Client includes any individual, organisation, department or division, including any belonging to the same organisation as the research agency which is responsible for commissioning a research project.
- **Agency**
  Agency includes any individual, organisation, department or division, including any belonging to the same organisation as the client which is responsible for, or acts as, a supplier on all or part of a research project.
- **Professional Body**
  Professional body refers to The Market Research Society.
- **Public Place**
  A 'public place' is one to which the public has access (where admission has been gained with or without a charge) and where an individual could reasonably expect to be observed and/or overheard by other people, for example in a shop, in the street or in a place of entertainment.

PRINCIPLES

Research is founded upon the willing co-operation of the public and of business organisations. It depends upon their confidence that it is conducted honestly, objectively, without unwelcome intrusion and without harm to respondents. Its purpose is to collect and analyse information, and not directly to create sales nor to influence the opinions of anyone participating in it. It is in this spirit that the Code of Conduct has been devised.

The general public and other interested parties shall be entitled to complete assurance that every research project is carried out strictly in accordance with this Code, and that their rights of privacy are respected. In particular, they must be assured that no information which could be used to identify them will be made available without their agreement to anyone outside the agency responsible for conducting the research. They must also be assured that the information they supply will not be used for any purposes other than research and that they will not be adversely affected or embarrassed as a direct result of their participation in a research project.

Wherever possible respondents must be informed as to the purpose of the research and the likely length of time necessary for the collection of the information. Finally, the research findings themselves must always be reported accurately and never used to mislead anyone, in any way.

RULES

A. Conditions of Membership and Professional Responsibilities

A.1 Membership of the professional body is granted to individuals who are believed, on the basis of the information they have given, to have such qualifications as are specified from time to time by the professional body and who have undertaken to accept this Code of Conduct. Membership may be withdrawn if this information is found to be inaccurate.

General responsibilities

A.2 Members shall at all times act honestly in dealings with respondents, clients (actual or potential), employers, employees, subcontractors and the general public.

A.3 Members shall at all times seek to avoid conflicts of interest with clients or employers and shall make prior voluntary and full disclosure to all parties concerned of all matters that might give rise to such conflict.

A.4   The use of letters after an individual's name to indicate member-ship of The Market Research Society is permitted in the case of Fellows (FMRS) and Full Members (MMRS). All members may point out, where relevant, that they belong to the appropriate category of the professional body.

A.5   Members shall not imply in any statement that they are speak-ing on behalf of the professional body unless they have the written authority of Council or of some duly delegated individual or committee.

Working practices

A.6   Members shall ensure that the people (including clients, colleagues and subcontractors) with whom they work are sufficiently familiar with this Code of Conduct and that working arrangements are such that the Code is unlikely to be breached through ignorance of its provisions.

A.7   Members shall not knowingly take advantage, without permis-sion, of the unpublished work of a fellow member which is the property of that member. Specifically, members shall not carry out or commission work based on proposals prepared by a mem-ber in another organisation unless permission has been obtained from that organisation.

A.8   All written or oral assurances made by anyone involved in com-missioning of conducting projects must be factually correct and honoured.

Responsibilities to other members

A.9   Members shall not place other members in a position in which they might unwittingly breach any part of this Code of Conduct.

Responsibilities of clients to agencies

A.10   Clients should not normally invite more than four agencies to tender in writing for a project. If they do so, they should disclose how many invitations to tender they are seeking.

A.11   Unless paid for by the client, a specification for a project drawn up by one research agency is the property of that agency and may not be passed on to another agency without the permission of the originating research agency.

Confidential survey research and other activities

(apply B.15 and Notes to B.15)

A.12 Members shall only use the term *confidential survey research* to describe research projects which are based upon respondent anonymity and do not involve the divulgence of identities or personal details of respondents to others except for research purposes.

A.13 If any of the following activities are involved in, or form part of, a project then the project lies outside the scope of confidential survey research and must not be described or presented as such:

(a) enquiries whose objectives include obtaining personal information about private individuals per se, whether for legal, political, supervisory (e.g. job performance), private or other purposes;

(b) the acquisition of information for use by credit-rating or similar purposes;

(c) the compilation, updating or enhancement of lists, registers or databases which are not exclusively for research purpose (e.g. which will be used for direct or relationship marketing);

(d) industrial, commercial or any other form of espionage;

(e) sales or promotional responses to individual respondents;

(f) the collection of debts;

(g) fund raising;

(h) direct or indirect attempts, including the framing of questions, to influence a respondent's opinions or attitudes on any issue other than for experimental purposes which are identified in any report or publication of the results.

A.14 Where any such activities referred to by paragraph A.13 are carried out by a member, the member must clearly differentiate such activities by:

(a) not describing them to anyone as confidential survey research and

(b) making it clear to respondents at the start of any data collection exercise what the purposes of the activity are and that the activity is not confidential survey research.

Scope of Code

A.15 When undertaking confidential survey research based on respondent anonymity, members shall abide by the ICC/ESOMAR

International Code of Conduct which constitutes Section B of this Code.

A.16 MRS Guidelines issued, other than those published as consultative drafts, are binding on members where they indicate that actions or procedures *shall or must* be adhered to by members. Breaches of these conditions will be treated as breaches of the Code and may be subject to disciplinary action.

A.17 Recommendations within such guidelines that members should behave in certain ways are advisory only.

A.18 It is the responsibility of members to keep themselves updated on changes or amendments to any part of this Code which are published from time to time and announced in publications and on the Web pages of the Society. If in doubt about the interpretation of the Code, members may consult the Professional Standards Committee or its Codeline Service set up to deal with Code enquiries.

Disciplinary action

A.19 Complaints regarding breaches of the Code of Conduct by those in membership of the MRS must be made to The Market Research Society.

A.20 Membership may be withdrawn, or other disciplinary action taken, if, on investigation of a complaint, it is found that in the opinion of the professional body, any part of the member's research work or behaviour breaches this Code of Conduct.

A.21 Members must make available the necessary information as and when requested by the Professional Standards Committee and Disciplinary Committee in the course of an enquiry.

A.22 Membership may be withdrawn, or other disciplinary action taken, if a member is deemed guilty of unprofessional conduct. This is defined as a member:

(a) being guilty of any act or conduct which in the opinion of a body appointed by Council might bring discredit on the profession, the professional body or its members;

(b) being guilty of any breach of the Code of Conduct set out in this document;

(c) knowingly being in breach of any other regulations laid down from time to time by the Council of the professional body;

(d) failing without good reason to assist the professional body in the investigation of a complaint;

(e) having a receiving order made against him/her or making any arrangement or composition with his/her creditors;

(f) being found to be in breach of the Data Protection Act by the Data Protection Registrar.

A.23 No member will have his/her membership withdrawn, demoted or suspended under this Code without an opportunity of a hearing before a tribunal, of which s/he will have at least one month's notice.

A.24 Normally, the MRS will publish the names of members who have their membership withdrawn, demoted or are suspended or have other disciplinary action taken with the reasons for the decision.

A.25 If a member subject to a complaint resigns his/her membership of the Society whilst the case is unresolved, then such resignation shall be published and in the event of re-admission to membership the member shall be required to co-operate in the completion of any outstanding disciplinary process.

B. ICC/ESOMAR Code of Marketing and Social Research Practice

General

B.1 Marketing research must always be carried out objectively and in accordance with established scientific principles.

B.2 Marketing research must always conform to the national and international legislation which applies in those countries involved in a given research project.

The rights of respondents

B.3 Respondents' co-operation in a marketing research project is entirely voluntary at all stages. They must not be misled when being asked for co-operation.

B.4 Respondents' anonymity must be strictly preserved. If the respondent on request from the Researcher has given permission for data to be passed on in a form which allows that respondent to be identified personally:

(a) the Respondent must first have been told to whom the information would be supplied and the purposes for which it will be used, and also

(b) the Respondent must ensure that the information will not be used for any non-research purpose and that the recipient of the information has agreed to conform to the requirements of the Code.

B.5 The Researcher must take all reasonable precautions to ensure that Respondents are in no way directly harmed or adversely affected as a result of their participation in a marketing research project.

B.6 The Researcher must take special care when interviewing children and young people. The informed consent of the parent or responsible adult must first be obtained for interviews with children.

B.7 Respondents must be told (normally at the beginning of the interview) if observation techniques or recording equipment are used, except where these are used in a public place. If a respondent so wishes, the record or relevant section of it must be destroyed or deleted. Respondents' anonymity must not be infringed by the use of such methods.

B.8 Respondents must be enabled to check without difficulty the identity and bona fides of the Researcher.

The professional responsibilities of researchers

B.9 Researchers must not, whether knowingly or negligently, act in any way which could bring discredit on the marketing research profession or lead to a loss of public confidence in it.

B.10 Researchers must not make false claims about their skills and experience or about those of their organisation.

B.11 Researchers must not unjustifiably criticise or disparage other Researchers.

B.12 Researchers must always strive to design research which is cost-efficient and of adequate quality, and then to carry this out to the specification agreed with the Client.

B.13 Researchers must ensure the security of all research records in their possession.

B.14 Researchers must not knowingly allow the dissemination of conclusions from a marketing research project which are not adequately supported by the data. They must always be prepared to make available the technical information necessary to assess the validity of any published findings.

B.15 When acting in their capacity as Researchers the latter must not undertake any non-research activities, for example database marketing involving data about individuals which will be used for direct marketing and promotional activities. Any such non-research activities must always, in the way they are organised and carried out, be clearly differentiated from marketing research activities.

Mutual rights and responsibilities of researchers and clients

B.16 These rights and responsibilities will normally be governed by a written Contract between the Researcher and the Client. The parties may amend the provisions of rules B.19 – B.23 below if they have agreed this in writing beforehand; but the other requirements of this Code may not be altered in this way. Marketing research must also always be conducted according to the principles of fair competition, as generally understood and accepted.

B.17 The Researcher must inform the Client if the work to be carried out for that Client is to be combined or syndicated in the same project with work for other Clients but must not disclose the identity of such clients without their permission.

B.18 The Researcher must inform the Client as soon as possible in advance when any part of the work for that Client is to be sub-contracted outside the Researcher's own organisation (including the use of any outside consultants). On request the Client must be told the identity of any such subcontractor.

B.19 The Client does not have the right, without prior agreement between the parties involved, to exclusive use of the Researcher's services or those of his organisation, whether in whole or in part. In carrying out work for different clients, however, the Researcher must endeavour to avoid possible clashes of interest between the services provided to those clients.

B.20 The following Records remain the property of the Client and must not be disclosed by the Researcher to any third party without the Client's permission:

(a) marketing research briefs, specifications and other information provided by the Client;

(b) the research data and findings from a marketing research project (except in the case of syndicated or multi-client projects or services where the same data are available to more than one client.

The Client has, however, no right to know the names or addresses of Respondents unless the latter's explicit permission for this has first been obtained by the Researcher (this particular requirement cannot be altered under Rule B.16).

B.21 Unless it is specifically agreed to the contrary, the following Records remain the property of the Researcher:

(a) marketing research proposals and cost quotations (unless these have been paid for by the Client). They must not be disclosed by the Client to any third party, other than to a consultant working for the Client on that project (with the exception of any consultant working also for a competitor of the Researcher). In particular, they must not be used by the Client to influence research proposals or cost quotations from other Researchers.

(b) the contents of a report in the case of syndicated research and/or multi-client projects or services when the same data are available to more than one client and where it is clearly understood that the resulting reports are available for general purchase or subscription. The Client may not disclose the findings of such research to any third party (other than his own consultants and advisors for use in connection with his business) without the permission of the Researcher.

(c) all other research Records prepared by the Researcher (with the exception in the case of non-syndicated projects of the report to the Client, and also the research design and questionnaire where the costs of developing these are covered by the charges paid by the Client).

B.22 The Researcher must conform to current agreed professional practice relating to the keeping of such records for an appropriate period of time after the end of the project. On request the Researcher must supply the Client with duplicate copies of such records provided that such duplicates do not breach anonymity and confidentiality requirements (Rule B.4); that the request is made within the agreed time limit for keeping the Records; and that the Client pays the reasonable costs of providing the duplicates.

B.23 The Researcher must not disclose the identity of the Client (provided there is no legal obligation to do so) or any confidential information about the latter's business, to any third party without the Client's permission.

B.24 The Researcher must, on request, allow the Client to arrange for checks on the quality of fieldwork and data preparation provided that the Client pays any additional costs involved in this. Any such checks must conform to the requirements of Rule B.4.

B.25 The Researcher must provide the Client with all appropriate technical details of any research project carried out for that Client.

B.26 When reporting on the results of a marketing research project the Researcher must make a clear distinction between the findings as such, the Researcher's interpretation of these and any recommendations based on them.

B.27 Where any of the findings of a research project are published by the Client, the latter has a responsibility to ensure that these are not misleading. The Researcher must be consulted and agree in advance the form and content of publication, and must take action to correct any misleading statements about the research and its findings.

B.28 Researchers must not allow their names to be used in connection with any research project as an assurance that the latter has been carried out in conformity with this Code unless they are confident that the project has in all respects met the Code's requirements.

B.29 Researchers must ensure that Clients are aware of the existence of this Code and of the need to comply with its requirements.

NOTES

How the ICC/ESOMAR International Code of Marketing and Social Research Practice should be Applied

These general notes published by ICC/ESOMAR apply to the interpretation of Section B of this Code in the absence of any specific interpretation which may be found in the MRS Definitions, in Part A of the MRS Code or in Guidelines published by the MRS. MRS members who are also members of ESOMAR will in addition be subject to requirements of the guidelines published by ESOMAR.

These Notes are intended to help users of the Code to interpret and apply it in practice.

The Notes, and the Guidelines referred to in them, will be reviewed and reissued from time to time. Any query or problem about how to apply the Code in a specific situation should be addressed to the Secretariat of MRS.

The rights of respondents

All Respondents entitled to be sure that when they agree to co-operate in any marketing research project they are fully protected by the provisions of this Code and that the Researcher will conform to its requirements. This applies equally to Respondents interviewed as private individuals and to those interviewed as representatives of organisations of different kinds.

Note on Rule B.3

Researcher and those working on their behalf (e.g. interviewers) must not, in order to secure Respondents' co-operation, make statements or promises which are knowingly misleading or incorrect – for example, about the likely length of the interview or about the possibilities of being re-interviewed on a later occasion. Any such statements and assurances given to Respondents must be fully honoured.

Respondents are entitled to withdraw from an interview at any stage and to refuse to co-operate further in the research project. Any or all of the information collected from or about them must be destroyed without delay if the Respondents so request.

Note on Rule B.4

All indications of the identity of Respondents should be physically separated from the records of the information they have provided as soon as possible after the completion of any necessary fieldwork quality checks. The Researcher must ensure that any information which might identify Respondents is stored securely, and separately from the other information they have provided; and that access to such material is restricted to authorised research personnel within the Researcher's own organisation for specific research purposes (e.g. field administration, data processing, panel or 'longitudinal' studies or other forms of research involving recall interviews).

To preserve Respondents' anonymity not only their names and addresses but also any other information provided by or about them which could in practice identify them (e.g. their Company and job title) must be safeguarded.

These anonymity requirements may be relaxed only under the following safeguards:

(a) Where the Respondent has given explicit permission for this under the conditions of 'informed consent' summarised in Rule 4 (a) and (b).
(b) where disclosure of names to a third party (e.g. a Subcontractor) is essential for any research purpose such as data processing or further interview (e.g. an independent fieldwork quality check) or for further follow-up research. The original Researcher is responsible for ensuring that any such third party agrees to observe the requirements of this Code, in writing, if the third party has not already formally subscribed to the Code.

It must be noted that even these limited relaxations may not be permissible in certain countries. The definition of 'non-research activity', referred to in Rule 4(b), is dealt with in connection with Rule 15.

Note on Rule B.5

The Researcher must explicitly agree with the Client arrangements regarding the responsibilities for product safety and for dealing with any complaints or damage arising from faulty products or product misuse. Such responsibilities will normally rest with the Client, but the Researcher must ensure that products are correctly stored and handled while in the Researcher's charge and that Respondents are given appropriate instructions for their use. More generally, Researchers should avoid interviewing at inappropriate or inconvenient times. They should also avoid the use of unnecessarily long interviews; and the asking of personal questions which may worry or annoy Respondents, unless the information is essential to the purposes of the study and the reasons for needing it are explained to the Respondent.

Note on Rule B.6

The definitions of 'children' and 'young people' may vary by country but if not otherwise specified locally should be taken as 'under 14 years' and '14–17 years' (under 16, and 16–17 respectively in the UK).

Note on Rule B.7

The Respondent should be told at the beginning of the interview that recording techniques are to be used unless this knowledge might bias the Respondent's subsequent behaviour: in such cases the Respondent must be told about the recording at the end of the interview and be given the opportunity to see or hear the relevant section of the record and, if they so wish, to have this destroyed. A 'public place' is defined as one to which the public has free access and where an individual could reasonably expect to be observed and/or overheard by other people present, for example in a shop or in the street.

Note on Rule B.8

The name and address/telephone number of the Researcher must normally be made available to the Respondent at the time of interview. In cases where an accommodation address or 'cover name' are used for data collection purposes arrangements must be made to enable Respondents subsequently to find without difficulty or avoidable expense the name and address of the Researcher. Wherever possible 'Freephone' or similar facilities should be provided so that Respondents can check the Researcher's bona fides without cost to themselves.

The professional responsibilities of researchers

This Code is not intended to restrict the rights of Researchers to undertake any legitimate marketing research activity and to operate competitively in so doing. However, it is essential that in pursuing these objectives the general public's confidence in the integrity of marketing research is not undermined in any way. This Section sets out the responsibilities which the Researcher has towards the public at large and towards the marketing research profession and other members of this.

Note on Rule B.14

The kinds of technical information which should on request be made available include those listed in the Notes to Rule B.25. The Researcher must not however disclose information which is confidential to the Client's business, nor need he/she disclose information relating to parts of the survey which were not published.

Note on Rule B.15

The kinds of non-research activity which must not be associated in any way with the carrying out of marketing research include: enquiries whose objectives are to obtain personal information about private individuals per se, whether for legal, political, supervisory (e.g. job performance), private or other purposes; the acquisition of information for use for credit-rating or similar purposes; the compilation, updating or enhancement of lists, registers or databases which are not exclusively for research purposes (e.g. which will be used for direct marketing); industrial, commercial or any other form of espionage; sales or promotional attempts to individual Respondents; the collection of debts; fund-raising; direct or indirect attempts, including by the design of the questionnaire, to influence a Respondent's opinions, attitudes or behaviour on any issue.

Certain of these activities – in particular the collection of information for databases for subsequent use in direct marketing and similar operations – are legitimate marketing activities in their own right. Researchers (especially those working within a client company) may often be involved with such activities, directly or indirectly. In such cases it is essential that a clear distinction is made between these activities and marketing research since by definition marketing research anonymity rules cannot be applied to them.

Situations may arise where a Researcher wishes, quite legitimately, to become involved with marketing database work for direct marketing (as distinct from marketing research) purposes: such work must not be carried out under the name of marketing research or of a marketing research Organisation as such.

The mutual rights and responsibilities of researchers and clients

This Code is not intended to regulate the details of business relationships between Researchers and Clients except in so far as these may involve principles of general interest and concern. Most such matters should be regulated by the individual business. It is clearly vital that such Contracts are based on an adequate understanding and consideration of the issues involved.

Note on Rule B.18

Although it is usually known in advance what subcontractors will be used, occasions do arise during the project where subcontractors need to be brought in, or changed, at very short notice. In such cases, rather than cause delays to the project in order to inform the Client it will usually be sensible and acceptable to let the Client know as quickly as possible after the decision has been taken.

Note on Rule B.22

The period of time for which research Records should be kept by the Researcher will vary with the nature of the project (e.g. ad hoc, panel, repetitive) and the possible requirements for follow-up research or further analysis. It will normally be longer for the stored research data resulting from a survey (tabulations, discs, tapes etc.) than for primary field records (the original completed questionnaires and similar basic records). The period must be disclosed to, and agreed by, the Client in advance. In default of any agreement to the contrary, in the case of ad hoc surveys the normal period for which the primary field records should be retained is one year after completion of the fieldwork while the research data should be stored for possible further analysis for at least two years. The Researcher should take suitable precautions to guard against any accidental loss of the information, whether stored physically or electronically, during the agreed storage period.

Note on Rule B.24

On request the Client, or his mutually acceptable representative, may observe a limited number of interviews for this purpose. In certain cases, such as panels or in situations where a Respondent might be known to (or be in subsequent contact with) the Client, this may require the previous agreement of the Respondent. Any such observer must agree to be bound by the provisions of this Code, especially Rule B.4.

The Researcher is entitled to be recompensed for any delays and increased fieldwork costs which may result from such a request. The Client must be informed if the observation of interviews may mean that the results of such interviews will need to be excluded from the overall survey analysis because they are no longer methodologically comparable.

In the case of multi-client studies the Researcher may require that any such observer is independent of any of the Clients.

Where an independent check on the quality of the fieldwork is to be carried out by a different research agency the latter must conform in all respects to the requirements of this Code. In particular, the anonymity of the original Respondents must be fully safeguarded and their names and addresses used exclusively for the purposes of back-checks, not being disclosed to the Client. Similar considerations apply where the Client wishes to carry out checks on the quality of data preparation work.

Notes on Rule B.25

The Client is entitled to the following information about any marketing research project to which he has subscribed:

(1) Background
- for whom the study was conducted
- the purpose of the study
- names of subcontractors and consultants performing any substantial part of the work

(2) Sample
- a description of the intended and actual universe covered
- the size, nature and geographical distribution of the sample (both planned and achieved); and where relevant, the extent to which any of the data collected were obtained from only part of the sample
- details of the sampling method and any weighting methods used
- where technically relevant, a statement of response rates and a discussion of any possible bias due to non-response

(3) Data collection
- a description of the method by which the information was collected
- a description of the field staff, briefing and field quality control methods used
- the method of recruiting Respondents; and the general nature of any incentives offered to secure their co-operation
- when the fieldwork was carried out
- (in the case of 'desk research') a clear statement of the sources of the information and their likely reliability

(4) Presentation of results
- the relevant factual findings obtained
- bases of percentages (both weighted and unweighted)
- general indications of the probable statistical margins of error to be attached to the main findings, and the levels of statistical significance of differences between key figures
- the questionnaire and other relevant documents and materials used (or, in the case of a shared project, that portion relating to the matter reported on).

The Report on a project should normally cover the above points or provide a reference to a readily available document which contains the information.

Note on Rule B.27

If the Client does not consult and agree in advance the form of publication with the Researcher the latter is entitled to:

(a) refuse permission for his name to be used in connection with the published findings and
(b) publish the appropriate technical details of the project (as listed in the Notes to B.25).

Note on Rule B.29

It is recommended that Researchers specify in their research proposals that they follow the requirements of this Code and that they make a copy available to the Client if the latter does not already have one.

CODELINE

Codeline is a free, confidential answer service to Market Research Society Code of Conduct related queries raised by market researchers, clients, respondents and other interested parties. The aim of Codeline is to provide an immediate, personal and practical interpretation and advice service.

Codeline is directly responsible to the MRS Professional Standards Committee (PSC) to which each query and its response is reported at PSC's next meeting. Queries from enquirers are handled by an individual member of the Codeline panel, drawn from past members of the PSC. As long as contact can be made with the enquirer, queries will be dealt with by Codeline generally within 24 hours. Where necessary, the responding Codeline member can seek further specialist advice.

Codeline's response to enquirers is not intended to be definitive but is the personal interpretation of the individual Codeline member, based on personal Code-related experience. PSC and Codeline panellists may highlight some of the queries and responses for examination and ratification by the PSC, the ultimate arbiter of the Code, at its next meeting. In the event that an individual Codeline response is not accepted by the PSC the enquirer will be notified immediately.

Enquirer details are treated as totally confidential outside the PSC but should 'Research' or any other MRS journal wish to refer to a particularly interesting or relevant query in 'Problem Page' or similar, permission is sought and obtained from the enquirer before anonymous publication and after that query's examination by PSC.

Codeline operates in the firm belief that a wide discussion of the issues arising from queries or anomalies in applying the Code and its associated guidelines within the profession will lead both to better understanding, awareness and application of the Code among members and to a better public appreciation of the ethical standards the market research industry professes and to which it aspires.

How to use Codeline

Codeline deals with any market research ethical issues. To contact Codeline please phone or fax the MRS Secretariat who will then allocate your query to a Codeline panellist.

If you choose to contact MRS by phone, the MRS Secretariat will ask you to confirm by fax the nature of your query, whether or not the caller is an MRS member or works for an organisation which employs an MRS member and a phone number at which you can be contacted. This fax will then be sent to the allocated panellist who will discuss your query directly with you by phone as soon as possible after receipt of your enquiry.

Please forward any queries about the MRS Code of Conduct and Guidelines, in writing to the:

MRS Secretariat, 15 Northburgh Street, London EC1V OJR
Tel: 020 7490 4911; Fax: 020 7490 0608

NOTES

1. In particular shall not be processed unless at least one of the conditions in Schedule 2 is met, and in the case of sensitive data, at least one of the conditions of Schedule 3 is also met. (These schedules provide that in determining whether personal data has been processed fairly, consideration must be given to the basis on which it was obtained.)

Glossary of market research terms

It is always of concern to management that the advertising, research and computer sectors are full of jargon. You have to be in the knowledge to be able to use this jargon, and if used incorrectly it can almost contribute to your becoming alienated and not accepted among the users of the specialist techniques. Therefore, I felt it worthwhile to list the key research jargon and to identify the usefulness of the techniques described. This glossary, therefore, is the key checklist of everything a manager must know in order to use and perform with research effectively – and be seen to be 'in the know-how' of research.

Attitude statements   A psychological concept designed to evaluate and investigate values, beliefs and motives for different forms of behaviour. Developing statements to describe your company and its products and services compared with those of your competitors provides the means of creating a control, asking consumers whether they agree or disagree with the attitudes and, in time, monitoring the changes.

Cluster analysis   A technique of multivariate analysis, which identifies groups of individuals that are similar to and different from each other. It is a way of establishing whether a group of people have similar attitudes or characteristics, which help to define or confirm subsegments of a market. It is an important technique for defining which types of product suit different types of consumer, and also establishing whether communications can be developed for specific market segments.

Conjoint analysis A method of evaluating consumer preferences among product concepts, which vary in respect of several attributes, based on asking people to rank those they most and least prefer. Using this analysis helps to develop data on how certain types of customer have a preference for purchasing and using certain types of product. It will therefore define what is the ideal product for customers because of how well the product meets their needs.

Demographics Sex, age and social grade are the key parts of the classification data in research, and comprise the demographics of the market being researched. It is vital for defining a market initially to know who are the current and potential customers. This becomes the basic benchmark data on which psychographic analyses are developed and created. The Market Research Society published the 5th Edition of *Occupations Groupings: A Job Dictionary* in 2002 (ISBN 0–9061–1727–5). The following is extracted as the key information for survey users:

Occupation Groups

The Occupation Groups are as follows:

A Approximately 3% of the total population. These are professional people, very senior managers in business or commerce or top-level civil servants. Retired people, previously grade A, and their widows.

B Approximately 20% of the population. Middle management executives in large organizations, with appropriate qualifications. Principal officers in local government and civil service. Top management or owners of small business concerns, educational and service establishments. Retired people, previously grade B, and their widows.

C1 Approximately 28% of the total population. Junior management, owners of small establishments, and all others in non-manual positions. Jobs in this group have very varied responsibilities and educational requirements. Retired people, previously grade C1 and their widows.

C2 Approximately 21% of the population. All skilled manual workers, and those manual workers with responsibility for other people. Retired people, previously C2, with pensions from their job. Widows, if receiving pensions from their late husband's job.

D Approximately 18% of the population. All semi-skilled and unskilled manual workers, apprentices and trainees to skilled workers. Retired people, previously grade D, with pensions from their job. Widows, if receiving a pension from their late husband's job.

E Approximately 10% of the population. All those entirely dependent on the state long-term, through sickness, unemployment, old age or other reasons. Those unemployed for a period exceeding six months. Casual workers and those without a regular income. Only households without a Chief Income Earner will be coded in this group.

Grading on Occupation
In the majority of cases, the decision as to whose occupation to use for grading is very simple.

- Social grading based on occupation of Head of Household, or
- Social grading based on Chief Income Earner.

Desk research   This is based on the use of secondary data, collecting published information relevant to the company's markets and products. Collection of this information may be important in understanding markets and can help to design survey research, in particular to prevent the survey duplicating the collection of data that is already available.

Family life cycles   Stages in the development of families: young single people and young couples, the early stage; couples with children at home, the mid-life stage; and older people without children, the late stage.

Forecasting   Estimating the probability of an event in the future. It may also be a prediction mode using a mathematical model, or from an extrapolation of current trends. This is important as a technique in a defined market, which can be tracked by monitoring key facts, habits and activities of the market that has been classified. It is particularly useful as a way of analysing products and product performances if product design or formulation is changed to alter the market or sales in the market.

Geodemographics   A method of classifying households based on multivariate analysis of data from the Census of Population. The practical application of geodemographic classifications generally depends on computer matching addresses to district classifications by means of the postcode. The application of geodemographics is useful for direct marketing, retail planning, or developing promotions and specific marketing activities for monitoring markets or ethnic groups.

Image statements   Consumers' perceptions or impressions of a company, product or service expressed in a clear statement. These are used to establish how close to or far away its ideas, concepts and strategies are from consumer needs.

Market mapping   A 'map' which shows the relative positions of the products in the market, consumers' or consumer characteristics. It is the most effective method for summarizing the findings of attitude research. There are two applications for market mapping. The first is literally to draw up the structure of the market and to add to the map the facts about each level of the market: the volume of sales, the classification of the customer types and so on. It is particularly good for understanding a market more clearly. The second is to use the analysis of survey research and to plot on a map the relationship between the defined customer types and the way in which attitudes are described or product attributes are rated. It is good for developing a product or communications strategy in sophisticated markets where it is important to develop strategies to respond to consumers' changing and demanding needs to counter competitive threats.

Market segmentation   Using classifications or market facts to divide a market into the characteristics of the product or service, user and buyer in the market, type or size of company. A central and very important marketing technique, market segmentation is a key tool to making research useful to grow business. It allows customer types and their different needs to be analysed, interpreted and monitored effectively. It assists in understanding how the market divides and how customers behave in different ways with different needs.

Marketing information system   All the information available to management, together with the hardware for its storage, processing and retrieval. Market intelligence, reports from all departments and market research are all part of this system. Creating, using and monitoring such a system is important for making the organization customer oriented.

Modelling   A model is a summary of observations, including mathematical models. It is a way of imitating or copying the market forces and testing out changes in a market, then observing the effects that result. It is a technique that is particularly effective in product and service research. It helps to anticipate market changes and move quickly once the effects of competitors' activity are reanalysed in the model.

Multivariate techniques   Those techniques that examine the relationships among a number of variables. They include analysis of variance, multi-regression, factor and principal component analysis, cluster analysis and discriminant analysis. Application of these techniques to survey analysis provides the manager with the opportunity to advance product and communications planning. It helps to translate the methods of marketing into the language and behaviour of consumers.

Paired comparison test   A test to compare two products or samples, with the purpose of getting a user or buyer to discriminate between them or identify changes or improvements. It is an important way of developing data to identify users' and buyers' attitudes to competitors' products and establish consumers' perceived benefits of your own.

Psychographic analysis   A segmentation application that classifies people into groups based on their behaviour or attitudes. It is becoming more and more important as a technique as it helps to classify and group the customers in a market, reflecting their needs in the context of their preferences and buying habits. It helps to make communications more direct and relevant, and to make market analysis more realistic in the context of getting to know the customer.

Regression analysis   A statistical method of calculating an equation which is applied to a set of bivariate or multivariate observations. It is a useful technique for analysing different market segments to identify whether any of the subgroups of customer have any similarities in behaviour, attitudes or preferences.

Sample   A representation of the whole, whose purpose is to enable investigation of the characteristics of the population. It is comprised of parts or subsets of the population being researched. Survey research depends on getting this right, as a survey completed with the wrong type of population is worthless.

Sampling   The technique for selecting a sample. It depends on setting up a sampling frame and identifying sampling units, which comprise a population. Survey research is only successful if this is completed well.

Trade-off models   A technique to discover the most attractive combination of attributes for a product or service, by the respondent expressing a preference for one or other alternative. An important technique for understanding clearly why people buy, how they evaluate whether the product or service that is offered corresponds with their needs, and the way in which they decide on making the purchase.

Index